Making Learning Happen

Strategies for an
Interactive Classroom

Jeffrey N. Golub
University of South Florida

Boynton/Cook Publishers
Heinemann
Portsmouth, NH

For my students

Boynton/Cook Publishers, Inc.
A subsidiary of Reed Elsevier Inc.
361 Hanover Street
Portsmouth, NH 03801–3912
www.boyntoncook.com

Offices and agents throughout the world

The author and publisher wish to thank those who have generously given permission to reprint borrowed material:

Excerpt from *Assessing English: Helping Students to Reflect on Their Work* by Brian Johnston. © 1987. Published by Open University Press. Reprinted by permission of the author.
Excerpt from "Activities for an Interactive Classroom" by Jeffrey N. Golub. © 1994 by the National Council of Teachers of English. Reprinted with permission.
Excerpt from *Beyond Discipline: From Compliance to Community* by Alfie Kohn (ASCD, 1996). © 1996 by Alfie Kohn. Used with the author's permission.
Credit lines continued on page 112.

Library of Congress Cataloging-in-Publication Data
Golub, Jeffrey N., 1944–
     Making learning happen : strategies for an interactive classroom / Jeffrey N. Golub.
         p.   cm.
     Includes bibliographical references and index.
     ISBN 0-86709-493-1
     1. English language—Study and teaching (Secondary)—United
States.   2. Education, Secondary—Activity program—United States.
     I. Title.
     LB1631.G623   1999
428'.0071'273—dc21   99-42070
                                                                CIP

Editor: Lisa Luedeke
Production: Elizabeth Valway
Cover design: Darci Mehall/Aureo Design
Manufacturing: Louise Richardson

Printed in the United States of America on acid-free paper
04   03   02   01   00   RRD   1   2   3   4   5

Contents

List of Figures

Foreword

Parents know kids make learning happen by constantly engaging the world through a multitude of activities. This engagement allows the cartoonist Bill Keane to portray kids as continually controlling their world in "Family Circus." They often take circuitous routes to achieve their tasks; they often try word combinations in new and different ways to the amazement of their parents—and the readers. They often come up with new and different perspectives on the same event. They make their own learning happen.

It is this kind of active learning that Jeffrey Golub replicates in order to uncover learning within the structured format of the language arts classroom. My first encounter with Golub's approach to teaching—in a middle school English class in Kent, Washington—introduced me to his interactive teaching methods. I was amazed at the contrast between the students' enthusiastic engagement with the learning activity and their quiet reflections on what the activity meant to them. I was watching a learning community in action. This book is designed to help us create the conditions for learning by engaging students in their world. Both the new and practicing teacher will gain from Golub's experience in teaching to make learning happen.

Clearly, the focus of this book is on language and allowing students to improve their expressive skills of speaking and writing and their receptive skills of reading and listening. This integration of the language arts supports many position statements by the National Council of Teachers of English and the National Communication Association. Because this true integration rarely occurs in practice, this book provides a giant step in that direction for all of us. But more important than this significant milestone of integration is the way in which Golub achieves it. The activities flow from one skill to another seamlessly. Golub relieves us from the burdensome question "How do you motivate students?" with his emphasis on "engaging" students in all activities. The activities suggested are adaptable to whatever location in which one teaches. He even recommends substitutions to adapt activities to the teacher's "own geographical area."

Just as Golub's "Something Important" speech activity requires an exchange between the student listeners and the student speaker, the book foregrounds the many layers of meaning in each teaching activity Golub suggests. The focus of the "Something Important" activity is on building a classroom community. The activity is designed to build comfort levels and prepare students for later oral activities. This activity, which takes place in an atmosphere of acceptance, reveals the "invisible" learning engendered by a complex task. The author grounds his efforts at community building on essential concepts from Larry Sarbaugh and Alfie Kohn: Sarbough's idea that the teacher is "a coordinator of a communication environment" and Kohn's concern for creating tasks worth doing. He also uses Kolb, Rubin, and McIntyre's "learning cycle" model to help set a stage for this community building.

Golub encourages us to interact with students through extensive group work. The group work is not approached in a businesslike or industrial model that would train students to learn to work in teams for a greater profit. Rather, it is set up to encourage student reflection and to lessen the role of the teacher, whose singular reflection on the students' work would be limited in perspective.

In Chapter 5, "Speaking of Participles and Gerbils," we discover that Golub's basic approach to grammar also incorporates the community-building strategies and models of engagement that are the hallmark of this book. When we learn that students in his grammar course not only take the "final examination" on the first day of class but discuss the implications of such a test as well, we realize how essential both community and communication are among all members of the class, including the teacher. Just as the reader will see the multiple layers of meaning for the students, the reader will realize that there are multiple approaches to making learning happen.

When Francis Bacon said, "the duty and office of Rhetoric is to apply Reason to Imagination for the greater moving of the will" (Dick 1955, 390), he identified an important part of learning: working with the imagination. This book is distinctive in that it encourages students to use their imaginations in many different ways and in the context of both the rich culture of our heritage and the realities of modern life. Golub promotes activities from creative drama to help with listening. While the primary goal here may be to build listening skills, use of one's imagination is clearly being encouraged as well. Many of the activities that Golub provides are springboards into the world of the imagination.

As readers we have the good fortune of feeling that we are in his methods class and he is talking to us. The flow of his personal style teaches us. Throughout this book, Golub insists that the teacher model activities for the student, as he does by giving the "Something Important" presentation himself to model the nature and length of the activity and making his own "Wanted" poster model, which reveals his love of chocolate. Modeling helps students eventually reflect on Golub's key questions for all his students: "What did you learn?" and "How do you know?" In the last chapter we see how he models teaching approaches to his own methods students by actually teaching lessons in the different classrooms in which they are doing their student teaching.

To demonstrate how to reach these goals, Golub provides readers with "The World's Simplest Lesson Plan" in the final chapter of the book. Yet the complexity of this "simple plan" is quickly revealed. Golub provides a series of questions for creating lesson plans that are creative, imaginative, and deep. We watch him struggle to find answers to his own four questions: (1) Where do you want to go?, (2) Why do you want to go there?, (3) How will you get there?, and (4) How will you know when you have arrived? His response when a lesson does not work is to revise or abandon it, but never without pushing forward to find a new and better way to help his students learn.

A major criticism of such approaches is often that they "abandon the past." Yet in these models, one quickly sees how he engages students with the use of such favorites as *Romeo and Juliet*, *Aesop's Fables*, *The Velveteen Rabbit*, "Grass," "Beat! Beat! Drums," and "Dulce et Decorum Est."

The energy of this book is fuel for the reader. Golub's teacher audience members will be eager for their next class session just so they can try one of these activities. This book is not a critique of current teaching but rather a map of new directions. This map's power is in its identification of those bumps and diversions that lie ahead. But it also provides teachers with a vision of those mountain peaks of significant learning.

Don M. Boileau
Professor of Speech Communication
George Mason University
Fairfax Station, VA

Work Cited

Dick, Hugh C., ed. 1955. *Selected Writings of Francis Bacon*. New York: Modern Library.

Acknowledgments

Several friends and colleagues helped me bring this manuscript to publication, and I am grateful to them all. Lois Bridges, Elizabeth Valway, and Lisa Luedeke, my editors at Heinemann Publishers, gave me considerable encouragement and support, and I thank all three of them for believing in me and my work. Lynne Mehley at Heinemann was extremely helpful and efficient in her pursuit of the permissions and sources I needed, and she helped keep me organized. I couldn't have done all that detail work without her help, since my own organizational style is best described as "abstract-bewildered." I owe her chocolate for this one.

After completing the major part of the manuscript, I turned to outside reviewers for advice and feedback. I asked two former methods students, Leslie Janos and Michael Vokoun, for help with this revising effort, and they offered tremendous assistance. Leslie and Michael both teach at Independent Day School in Tampa, and they do outstanding work in the classroom. They spent so many hours, days, and even whole weekends poring over the chapters, checking the text for clarity and completeness. The manuscript was made significantly "new and improved" because of their care and work, and I thank them sincerely.

Roy Alin and Don Boileau also read the manuscript and offered insightful comments and suggestions for revision. Roy supervised my student-teaching internship in Seattle, Washington, in 1967, and we have been close friends and colleagues ever since. Don Boileau, chairman of the Department of Speech Communication at George Mason University, has been my friend and mentor for almost thirty years now, and his comments and insights are always valuable. Thank you, gentlemen.

My thanks and appreciation to Gloria Rosenthal, both for her friendship and for her permission to reprint her cleverly constructed punctuation puzzle that appears at the beginning of Chapter 5.

My greatest appreciation to my wife, Martha, who put up with so much, from my constant requests to read passages and parts of the manuscript to many late nights of my writing and revising. Her comments and reflections helped me see things much more clearly.

And finally, to my students at the university, who endure all these strange and unnatural activities in the methods and graduate classes and then go out there and make learning happen for their own students in wonderfully challenging, engaging, and effective ways: This book is for you.

Introduction

In more than twenty years of trying to make learning happen for my students in both junior and senior high school classrooms, I have come to understand the cautionary note voiced by my mentor and respected colleague, Roy Alin: "Don't mistake *motion* for *progress*." Oh, we can keep our students *busy* in the classroom. That's no problem. They will fill out the worksheets and fill in the blanks and write up this and write down that . . . That's *motion*. But where's the *progress*? How can we—and our students—tell that something positive and productive and lasting has happened as a result of all this instructional "motion"? What elements of lesson planning and instruction are needed to ensure that *learning* happens?

That is what this book is about. It's about those elements needed to make learning happen. It does not ask you to stop doing what you are doing in the classroom and start doing something else entirely. Nor does it require that you throw away everything you have learned and, instead, learn something new. Rather, it describes and demonstrates ways to *restructure your classroom instruction* so that *progress* happens—so that your students will learn in engaging and effective ways.

The first chapter emphasizes the importance of *reflection* as a strategy to make students' invisible learning visible to them. Through reflection on their language performance, students become aware of their language habits and their level of skill in such processes as constructing and negotiating meanings. I describe several specific and exemplary activities to illustrate how this element of reflection may be used and integrated with your current classroom instruction.

In the second chapter, I present several activities that establish a sense of *community* in the classroom. This element is an integral part of making learning happen, and the activities described here will help you get started in designing your own community-building strategies.

Students' oral communication behavior is an important element of and accompaniment to their learning efforts in the classroom, so the third and fourth chapters deal with this aspect of classroom instruction. In Chapter 3, I describe activities that develop students' speaking and listening skills; and in Chapter 4, I present strategies to help students learn to work productively and harmoniously in a small-group setting.

In the fifth chapter, I show how all these elements—reflection, engagement, a sense of community, and students' oral communication behavior—work together in a restructured instructional approach to traditional English grammar. I chose this particular subject because the content is sometimes viewed as either dull or difficult. Through the use of such elements as I describe in the earlier chapters, even this aspect of the English curriculum can be made engaging and stimulating.

Finally, I outline "The World's Simplest Lesson Plan," a series of four questions that one must ask about any lesson, unit, or term project that one is designing. Coming up with satisfactory and valid responses to these questions is the best way to ensure that one's lessons and instructional strategies will indeed make learning happen for the students.

I designed this book to appeal to three different audiences: (1) experienced teachers will find classroom activities here that they can add to their own repertoire of instructional options to make learning happen; (2) beginning teachers will learn of the importance and value of integrating the elements of reflection, engagement, and community building into their lesson-planning efforts; and (3) university English methods instructors should find this volume a valuable accompaniment or supplement to their main text for their courses.

You may recognize some of the instructional activities in Chapters 3 and 4 dealing with oral communication. They are classic exercises that have been around for twenty-five years or more. I include them here for three reasons:

1. They still work.
2. English methods students and beginning teachers have not seen these activities before, and they need to know about them and how well these exercises can make learning happen in the classroom. Experienced teachers, in addition, may appreciate being reminded of the structure, value, and relevance of these activities.
3. For some of these classic exercises, I have designed variations in the procedures and directions or have described relevant follow-up activities that help make additional learning happen in this area of instruction.

The aim of this volume is to identify and describe those critical elements of classroom instruction that will make learning happen for your students in engaging and lasting ways. I hope that in reading and using this book, learning will happen for you, too.

1

Making Learning Happen

This is a book about making learning happen. But it's a certain *kind* of learning that I'm talking about—not the kind of learning that is measured by a standardized, multiple-choice test, nor the kind of learning that occurs on Monday but is gone by Friday. I'm not talking, either, of the stuff you have to "cover" in eighth grade in order to get the students ready for ninth grade. And I'm sure that standards and benchmarks and objectives and goals are all necessary somewhere and sometime, but not here and not now. Whatever the political goals of the district, this book is about making learning happen in your classroom.

I'm talking about *conscious* learning here, the kind of learning that enables students to assess the current level and quality of their language performance and then work to improve that performance deliberately, enthusiastically, and with commitment. Such learning cuts across all grade levels and all disciplines.

Making the Invisible Visible

The art of making learning happen involves making the invisible visible. Margaret Donaldson, in *Children's Minds* (1978), describes this concept in another way by saying:

> If the intellectual powers are to develop, the child must gain a measure of control over his own thinking, and he cannot control it while he remains unaware of it. (129)

If we are going to improve students' performance with language, we must first make the students *consciously aware* of the level and quality of that performance so that they can begin to "gain a measure of control" over it. We must make the invisible visible.

1

Reflecting on One's Work

Perhaps one of the most powerful and effective instructional strategies for helping students gain a measure of control over their own thinking and language performance is to have students engage in *reflection*. It is not enough for the student to have simply produced a required project, paper, or demonstration. He or she must be made consciously aware of what he or she did to produce such an artifact. If it is an outstanding effort, what elements contributed to its excellence? Or, if it is weak, why didn't it work? What went wrong? What needs to be changed or improved? Taking a step back and reflecting on one's performance can make such invisible insights visible. The goal is to become a reflective learner.

One might argue, however, that the most efficient way to help students become aware of their language performance is to simply *tell* them what they're doing right or wrong and send them on their way to the next assignment. But simply telling students the answer doesn't make learning happen—at least, not the kind of learning we're after—for a number of reasons:

1. Students' language performance is a complex phenomenon that doesn't change immediately or significantly simply because of teacher feedback. Such feedback can produce defensive behavior or discouragement instead of the desired improvement on subsequent coursework.

2. Certainly we want to make students' language performance "visible" to them so that they can make conscious decisions about the many substantive and stylistic options that confront them in their communication efforts. But we also want students to "own" their own learning, to care about it, and to use their emerging insights to engage in continual self-assessment. Making invisible language habits and behavior visible by our simply telling students the answers doesn't produce the kind of long-term, active commitment to one's own learning that reflecting on one's own work does.

3. Teacher intervention in the form of direct feedback can actually hinder or even stop entirely the students' own engagement in reflection. Brian Johnston, in his text *Assessing English: Helping Students to Reflect on Their Work* (1987), offers a clear and detailed description of the process of reflection and explains what goes wrong when teachers intervene too early:

   > To reflect upon one's own work is part of learning. Kolb, Rubin and McIntyre's "learning cycle" [see Figure 1–1] describes how an *active* learner *experiences* things, *reflects* on those experiences, *conceptualizes* what has been learnt and goes on to act on the basis of the conceptualization, that is, *experiments*.
   >
   > . . . School students have many experiences of writing, but I suspect that they reflect, conceptualize and experiment only rarely. When asked, "What

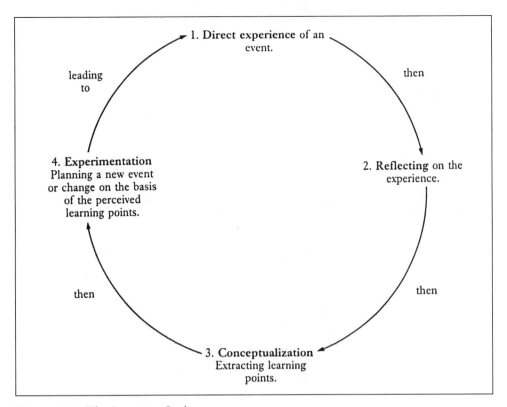

Figure 1–1. The Learning Cycle

did you learn from doing that writing?" or "What were you experimenting with?" students are often confused. The questions make little sense to them. If they cannot articulate what they are learning, then they are not learning in a way which is conscious and under their control.

If I am right that many students do not reflect, conceptualize and deliberately experiment in English lessons, we should be asking "Why not?" Part of the answer is that when teachers are expected to grade or mark each piece of work, then they do the reflecting and conceptualizing for the students. In many classes there is a gaping hole in the learning cycle [see Figure 1–2].

Students do the work, the teacher assesses it, the students look to see how the assessments compare with what they hoped for, and go straight on to the next experience without even rereading their work, let alone reflecting on it. Little wonder that many students make little progress in English in secondary school. (2–4)

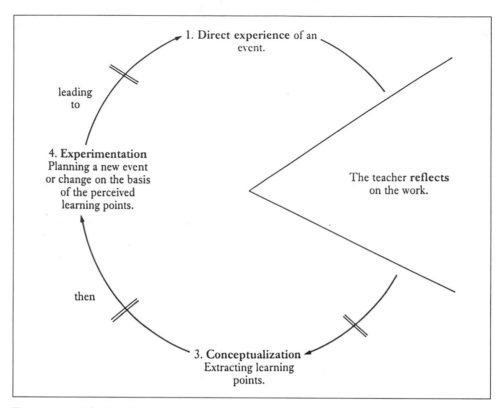

Figure 1–2. The Teacher Interrupts the Learning Cycle

To encourage students to engage in this process of reflection—indeed, to be willing to go through all of the stages of the learning cycle identified above—you need to lower the *risk factor* involved in such an activity. Students are not about to experiment with alternatives and options—to take risks in their language and communication efforts—if they are continually faced with the threat of a grade for every effort, every draft, every attempt, every time. So, lower the risk factor. Let the majority of your activities—and most of your students' work—be "rehearsals." Let students make mistakes, start over, revise often, and try out ideas, all in a classroom climate of experimentation and reflection.

Of course there will be times for a "performance," times when students need to demonstrate that they are now "new and improved" as a result of all of their rehearsals. These performances may be evaluated for a grade, but it's only fair to let students know well in advance when these performances will occur. Let them know also exactly which activities will be considered performances. Everything else—which should be most of the work most of the time—is risk-free rehearsal.

Making Reflecting Happen

Here is one way to engage students in reflecting on their work and thus make their invisible thinking visible to them: Imagine that your students have just finished working on a piece of writing, and they're about to hand it in for credit. It's a piece that has been drafted, shared with classmates in small groups, revised, edited, and finally made into a polished copy. This process has taken several days, and students are about to hand in a version that says, in effect, "Here's the best I can do with this piece at this time."

Then you say to your class, "Students, before you hand in your paper, would you take a few moments and respond in writing to one or more of the following questions:

- "What is it exactly that you tried to accomplish through this paper? How well do you think you accomplished it?
- "What do you like best about this writing that you have done? Which phrases or sections stand out in your mind as being particularly well-written?
- "What parts of your writing are you still concerned about? Perhaps these particular parts are not as clear or as vivid as you would like. Identify those parts and tell what it is about them that bothers you.
- "How did you get this writing done? Did you wait until almost the last minute and then write it all at once? Did you do extensive revising, or did you find that your rough draft was fairly clear and complete already?
- "What was the most difficult part of this assignment for you? What gave you the most trouble? How did you resolve this problem?
- "What grade do you think you have earned with this paper? Why do you think so?"

Such questions will engage students in reflecting on their writing efforts and help bring about a conscious awareness of the thinking that went into that effort. If students can become aware of what they're doing well—and what they need to improve—their subsequent performances can incorporate these important insights and lead to greater control. The students can retain what works and eliminate what doesn't.

Another example of an instructional activity that promotes reflective thinking comes from my English methods classes at the University of South Florida. In these classes, I prepare students who wish to teach English in middle and high schools. My goal in these courses is to challenge and change my students' assumptions about such fundamental questions as "What's worth knowing?" and "How do students learn?" To accomplish this goal, I employ a constructivist approach to teaching and learning—a philosophy of instruction that engages students in constructing their own knowledge instead of passively absorbing the knowledge of others. One of my methods courses requires the students to engage in a minimum of twenty-seven hours of observation in actual high school classrooms, so halfway through the course, I give the students this assignment:

> "For next week's class, bring in evidence from the classrooms you're observing that learning happened."

Usually at this point, students will raise several questions, seeking clarification and elaboration: "Do you mean . . . ?" "Are we supposed to . . . ?" "Does it have to be . . . ?" "Can you give us an example?" I decline to answer these questions and simply direct them to complete the assignment in any way they feel is appropriate, thus forcing them to create (construct) their own content and process answers.

At the next class session, we spend the entire three hours discussing and analyzing each student's item of evidence claiming to show that learning happened. One student will begin the discussion by saying, "Well, here's what I saw (or heard or found) in the classroom I observed, . . . " and other students are encouraged to ask questions and examine the evidence to determine if it does indeed show that learning happened. At appropriate times, additional students will volunteer their own evidence, and so the discussion and analysis proceeds. By the end of class, every student has presented his or her evidence and responded to the contributions of his or her classmates.

The assignment for the following week's class is "Write out your own theory of learning." And for the week after that, I direct students to turn their theory of learning into a fairy tale or fable.

This series of activities is designed to help students develop and articulate their own definition and theory of learning. Since they will soon be engaging in their teaching internships and will be trying to make learning happen for their own students, they need to construct a personal definition of learning that they can live with and teach with, and I do what I can to help them in this meaning-making effort. The first activity in the above sequence—Bring in evidence that learning happened—is designed to engage students in constructing their own meaning for the concept of "learning." They have to decide for themselves what constitutes learning—what it looks like when it happens and what evidence they might use to determine that learning did in fact occur. At the subsequent class session involving sharing and discussion and analysis of the various bits of evidence, the students engage in *negotiation of meanings*. One student presents his or her evidence, and classmates are encouraged to ask such probing questions as "How do you know that this evidence is valid?"

Through such negotiation of meanings, students' individual conceptions of learning are changed, modified, and improved. The final activity, requiring the students to turn their theory of learning into a fairy tale or fable, encourages them to refine their meaning-making effort by translating their conception from one symbolic system to another. They have an opportunity to view their conception of learning from a new angle and express their insights in a new way.

A distinguishing feature of the above series of activities is that the students' own talk is used as a vehicle for learning. Through the sharing and negotiation of meanings, students have an opportunity to learn from their classmates and revise their initial constructions. In this way also, their own, invisible thinking about this concept becomes visible to them, allowing them to gain a measure of control over it.

Imagine for a moment that *you* are asked to participate in this same exercise: Find evidence that learning happened in your own classroom today or this week or this semester or after the completion of the last composition or test or project. What evidence will you point to? A test score? The quality of the project or performance itself? A comment that a student made about the coursework or some other student behavior that you found particularly noteworthy? The kind of evidence you provide will say a lot about your own theory of learning and how you go about making learning happen for your students.

Let me suggest one way in which I might go about gathering such evidence. Remember that I want to engage students in reflection and make their invisible thinking visible to them. So, just after my class had completed a particular activity, project, or unit of study, I would hand out an index card to each student. Then I would say,

> "Students, I'm going to ask you to respond to a question in writing on this card. Write as much as you want, but write only on the front side of the card."
>
> And then I would pose the question: "What did you learn [from this assignment or project or unit of study]?"

After students had finished writing their responses, I would direct them to turn the card over and now write a response to this follow-up question: "How do you *know*? How do you know that you learned whatever it is that you listed on the front of the card?"

This is reflection. This is the students stepping back and looking hard at the activities they have just completed and mining them for whatever insights and other evidence of learning they may have picked up. This is the students making the invisible learning that has occurred visible to themselves. It is not enough that the students *performed* well on the last activity. I want each student to *know* that he or she did well, that he or she *learned* from the experience. I want the students to know that they know, and to know how they came to know it. And this culminating exercise—writing responses to the two questions "What did you learn?" and "How do you know?"—will help make these invisible insights visible to the students. It will also provide me with important evidence and information about whether learning did indeed happen.

Constructing and Negotiating Meanings

In dealing with literature, students at all levels of instruction should go through the whole learning cycle as outlined above. This means that they experience the text—sometimes through an oral reading in class, reading on their own or in small groups, listening to a recording of the text, or some other way—then reflect on the reading, perhaps through a response log or a small-group or whole-class discussion. The discussions with classmates allow students to try out their "rough-draft" ideas, to conceptualize and experiment with various interpretations and emerging insights.

This kind of learning involves students' ability to construct and negotiate meanings. In addition, I want to make the students *responsible* for the meanings they construct, so I'm continually reacting to their ideas and insights by asking such questions as "How do you know?" and "Where did you get that idea?" In response to such questions and probing, students are challenged to either defend and elaborate on their interpretations or modify or abandon them in favor of a "new and improved" idea.

This kind of ongoing constructing, reflecting, negotiating, and communicating of meanings occurs in a social context. It involves students in using their own classroom talk as a vehicle for learning—a basic characteristic of an interactive classroom.

To make this kind of learning happen, it is first important to establish the guidelines and procedures right at the beginning of a literary unit of study. I want my students to understand that if they're going to make sense of the texts we'll be reading together, they will have to do the majority of the necessary interpretive work. Oh, I'll be there to poke and probe and challenge and cajole. But their opinions count most: "The quality of the small-group and whole-class discussions in here will have a lot to do with the amount of *you* in them," I tell my students.

Second, I want my students to understand what is meant by the terms *constructing* and *negotiating* meanings, since they will be engaged in these processes throughout much of their coursework. So, to communicate the essence of these concepts, I conduct a brief introductory exercise with the students in constructing and negotiating meanings and let them *feel* what it's like to engage in these processes. This is simply another way of coming to know. I hand out a copy of the following parable to each student:

> Long ago in Japan the students in a certain school used to study meditation. Four of them who were close friends promised one another to observe seven days of silence.

On the first day all were silent. Their meditation had begun auspiciously, but when night came and the oil lamps were growing dim, one of the students could not help exclaiming to a servant: "Fix those lamps."

The second student was surprised to hear the first one talk: "We are not supposed to say a word," he remarked.

"You two are stupid. Why did you talk?" asked the third.

"I am the only one who has not talked," concluded the fourth student. (Reps 1998, 83–84)

I read the parable aloud, and then give these directions:

"Students, would you take a moment now and write down a moral—a lesson to be learned—for this story. Do not converse with your classmates first; just create a moral, write it down, and be done with it."

Note: If your students are younger, or you think they might have trouble understanding the concept of a moral, you might substitute one of Aesop's fables for the one above or perhaps use an Aesop fable and its moral as an introduction and example before this activity.

After allowing the students a few minutes to create and write down their morals, I give the next instructions:

"In just a moment, you are going to get together with a classmate, and the two of you are going to create a moral together. You can do this in one of four ways:

- "You read each other's moral and decide that person A has written a really good one, so you agree that that's the one you're going to use for this exercise. Fine! You're done.
- "Or you decide that person B has created an excellent moral that doesn't need any changes or improvements. You'll use that one.
- "You might decide to combine and rearrange parts of your two morals to create a new one.
- "Or perhaps after reading each other's lines, you decide that neither one is very good, so you draft a whole new moral together.

"Work with a partner in one of those four ways to create a moral together, and *those* are the morals that we will hear read aloud."

So the students work in pairs to create a moral that each partner likes, and about ten minutes later when everyone is finished, we hear their creations read aloud. Interesting reactions occur during the readings: there is laughter at this one, cries of "Oh, that's good!" after that one, murmurs of approval after most of them.

And then I explain: "This is what is meant by constructing and negotiating meanings. When you first worked alone to write a moral for this story, you were *constructing* a meaning, trying to make sense of the parable and express it in a concise statement. Then you got together with a partner and *negotiated* meanings. You compared your different interpretations and began to change your initial conception and perspective. Seeing your partner's interpretation either confirmed your belief in the accuracy and worth of your own moral or led you to see that perhaps there was something you were missing and that a revision was necessary. But you gained insight by talking with your partner and engaging in this negotiation process. And this is how we'll be making sense of the various texts we'll be reading in class—through this process of constructing and negotiating meanings.

"Now, I imagine that you might be sitting there wondering, 'But which moral is the *right* one?' or wondering what I, the teacher, came up with for a moral to this story. First, there *is* no right answer! If you liked best the moral that Leslie and Michael created together—if you think that one expresses best the lesson to be learned from this anecdote—then that's the right answer for you. And if someone else likes a different moral that he or she heard here, then that's the right one for him or her.

"I have deliberately refrained from giving you my own interpretation—my own response—to this story, for an important reason: if I were to say to you, 'Well, those morals you created together were pretty good, but now, here's mine,' then no matter how much you came to believe in an alternate interpretation, you would simply throw it away and seize upon mine because 'The teacher has spoken!' "

This is an important point to emphasize: None of this constructing, reflecting, negotiating, and communicating of meanings would occur if I were simply to give students the answers or play the "Guess What's in My Mind?" game with them:

> "Why do you think the main character acted that way on page fourteen?" . . . "No, that's not right. Try again? Anyone else want to guess?"

Students get really tired really fast of this "game" that teachers play. Their apathetic, disruptive, or even hostile behavior reflects their attitude of "Who cares? Just tell us the answer, Teacher!" Look again at Figure 1–2 of the Learning Cycle on page 4 and see what happens when the teacher intervenes with his or her own reflections and interpretations. It stops the students from doing their own thinking, constructing, and reflecting. Worse is that it stops most students from wanting to read good literature when the judgment is that their constructed meaning is wrong.

It stops the students from learning.

The "Three Questions" Activity

There are many instructional activities that engage students in constructing and negotiating meanings when dealing with literature, and I described some of them in a previous book, *Activities for an Interactive Classroom* (1994, 102–15). One of them is a basic, versatile activity that can serve well as a first exercise for students to encounter after the introductory experience above. This activity can be used with almost any kind of text, and it results in real engagement and significant learning for students. Here is how I described it previously in *Activities*:

> Asking questions about poetry is important, but it is the *students* who should be asking the questions as they seek to construct meanings. They should then collaborate with classmates to articulate their responses to those questions. The following activity provides a structure for this process:
>
> Introduce a poem to the class by first reading it aloud. Immediately ask students to write down three questions they have about the poem. These can be questions about a certain word ("What does this word mean?" "Why does the poet use this word here?"), a phrase, or a whole section. After the questions have been written, direct the students to form themselves into small groups, four or five people in each group. Then instruct the students to work within their groups to generate answers to their questions.
>
> This procedure has several advantages over a more traditional, teacher-led discussion: students are encouraged to ask their own questions of the poem instead of simply responding to the teacher's questions; this process uses students' talk as a vehicle for learning, allowing students to try out emerging ideas on each other; and a collaborative approach is used to generate individual meanings and insights.
>
> At the end of the small-group discussions, a recorder appointed for each group should summarize for the whole class what questions were brought up and what responses were generated. The entire class might then work together to provide additional responses and interpretations for those questions that a particular group found difficult to handle. You should find that, at the end of this process, the students will have covered—or more importantly, "UN-covered"—most of the points and parts of the poem that you, the teacher, would have discussed anyway. And they will have done it in a way that makes sense to them and allows them to make sense of the poem. (102–3)

This activity, in which the interpretive discussion of literature begins with the students' own questions, is, as I mentioned previously, a basic and versatile approach to engaging students in constructing and negotiating meanings. It can be used many times with many different texts—a chapter from a novel, a short story, a poem, a scene from a play—throughout the semester.

Additional Activities to Construct Meanings

There are other activities, of course, to engage students in this process of constructing meanings from a text, and I want to describe four of them here. These activities are appropriate for use with a wide variety of literature, especially short stories, novels, and poems that feature one or more characters.

For purposes of illustration, let's say that your students have just finished reading a certain chapter in a novel. You can begin a class discussion of the text with the "Three Questions" activity, of course, but don't stop there. Follow up with one or more of these activities:

Activity 1

"Imagine for a moment that this chapter depicts a series of scenes from a movie. What do you suppose the *next* scene will show? What will happen next in this movie? How will the movie end? Write your own, individual response first, and then we'll hear from volunteers and compare movies."

Activity 2

"Now imagine that we're actually going to produce the movie. Who would you cast to play [name of one of the featured characters]? It doesn't have to be a current actor, by the way. It can be a politician or sports star or TV personality or anyone else who you think would be *perfect* to portray this character."

One procedure that I have found effective for this second activity is to insist that the students *do not* call out the names that they think of in response to this question. If a student should yell out a name, it stops his or her classmates from doing their own thinking. Instead, I direct the students to simply write down their suggestion, and then we go around the room, and each student responds in turn. Often, we hear the same name repeated two or three times before we're finished, which is fine.

When everyone has named his or her suggestion, repeat this activity, this time casting other featured characters. Share responses as before.

Activity 3

"Let's consider the first character again for a moment. I'm going to ask you to respond to a question, and you will be tempted to yell out an answer immediately. *Don't* do that! Instead, simply write down your response, and then we'll go around the room and hear them all.

"Here's the question: If this character were *an item in a supermarket,* what item would he [or she] be? Be prepared to say why you chose that particular item."

After students have had a moment to write down a response, I give these directions:

"As we go around the room and hear from each person, please listen carefully to the various answers. If you hear a response that makes you wonder, 'Why did he or she choose *that* item?', write it down and after everyone has had a chance to contribute, you will have an opportunity to ask that person for the thinking behind his or her selection."

Sure enough, after all have had a chance to contribute, the students begin questioning their classmates: "Who said that the character would be a marshmallow?" The student who voiced that response is then invited to elaborate on his or her choice, identifying the similarities he or she perceives between the character and that particular item. In this way, students are encouraged to become responsible for their own meanings and constructions.

Some variations of this prompt include asking the students to see the character as

- a vehicle;
- a game;
- a sport;
- an animal;
- an item of furniture; or
- a weather condition (What kind of weather condition do you think Tybalt would be in *Romeo and Juliet?*).

Activity 4

"Write down a word or phrase from the chapter that captures the essence of this chapter for you. In a moment, we'll go around the room, hear what everyone has written, and then invite you to ask of your classmates, "Why did you choose *that* part?"

As a follow-up to the above activity, direct students to write down another word or phrase that captures the essence of this chapter for them but this time is *not* in the chapter. The sharing procedure is the same as before. This time the students are reading for the main idea and summarizing the essence or meaning of the chapter in their own words.

Common Characteristics of These Activities

All of the strategies described above engage students in constructing and negotiating meanings, helping students make sense of a text in ways that make sense to them. These strategies also share certain other characteristics. For instance, they all incorporate and exemplify the principles of an interactive classroom: students are performing with language; they are using their own talk as a vehicle for learning; they are communicating to a real audience for a real purpose; and the teacher is functioning as a designer and director of instruction.

This last principle—that the teacher serves as a designer and director, instead of as the main "actor" on stage—points to yet another common feature of all these strategies: in each of these activities, *the students talk more than the teacher does.* This important, defining characteristic of an interactive approach to instruction should be present in every exercise, every day. The teacher designs the instructional situation and then directs the students through it, but the *students* should be doing the talking. This is how one makes reflection happen . . . and learning, too.

It's how one makes the invisible visible to students.

Notes

You can find descriptions of several additional classroom activities that engage students in reflecting on their coursework and language performance in the volume that Louann Reid (Colorado State University, Fort Collins) and I co-edited titled *Reflective Activities: Helping Students Connect with Texts* (1999, Urbana, IL: National Council of Teachers of English).

Works Cited

Donaldson, M. 1978. *Children's Minds.* New York: W. W. Norton & Company.

Golub, J. N. 1994. *Activities for an Interactive Classroom.* Urbana, IL: National Council of Teachers of English.

Johnston, B. 1987. *Assessing English: Helping Students to Reflect on Their Work.* Epping, Australia: St. Clair.

Reps, P., ed. 1998. *Zen Flesh, Zen Bones: A Collection of Zen & Pre-Zen Writings.* Rutland, VT: Charles E. Tuttle.

2

Building a Sense of Community

A teacher is "a coordinator of a communication environment."[1] Many teachers overlook this important insight, but it is the key to establishing a sense of community and a positive classroom climate for learning. First, the classroom is a "communication environment." People *talk* in there. It's a *natural* place for talking: there are lots of people to talk with and lots of things to talk about. It's the teacher's job to *coordinate* or manage that talking, to design and structure procedures, situations, and activities that encourage students to talk about things worth talking about—and to ensure that all of this talking takes place in a climate of support and cooperation.

That's quite a job to do, establishing and managing a communication environment such as that. But, it can be done—and done well—if one attends to two critical elements involved in such an environment: (1) creating a climate of engagement and (2) building a sense of community, thus creating a place where the students feel "trusted and respected and empowered."[2] Let's deal with the engagement first.

Addressing a Common Concern

At the first session of my methods classes, I always ask the students to respond to this question: "What are you most concerned about as you prepare for your student-teaching internship next semester?" I ask this question because it gives students a chance to find out that they are not alone, that others are thinking similar thoughts and sharing the same fears and worries. It also gives me a chance to determine and address the students' specific interests and concerns.

One time a student mentioned a concern that many other students have also voiced over many semesters, but the way she phrased it made it memorable.

She said: "I'm afraid the students won't do what I *want* them to do."

That's a real concern there. And it's not only the methods students who are worried about it, either. Many experienced teachers, too, seek ways to make the students do what they want students to do—so *many* teachers, in fact, that a wealth of "classroom management" books and resources have appeared over the years, all describing and demonstrating "surefire" ways to get the students to comply with teachers' rules and demands.

But that's exactly the problem. Alfie Kohn, in his book *Beyond Discipline: From Compliance to Community* (1996), points out this basic flaw in almost every book on classroom discipline: they all describe a system or a set of procedures for making students *comply* with the teacher's demands. Essentially, they're saying to the teachers, "It doesn't matter what you're asking them to do or what assignments you're giving or how you want them to behave. I'll show you how to get them to *comply* with your rules and requests." It's always the *student's* fault if misbehavior occurs or the assignment is not completed.

Kohn, however, sees things differently. His whole approach is based on the assumption that (and this is my paraphrase), "If the students aren't doing what you want them to do, then maybe, just *maybe,* what you're asking them to do is not worth doing." In his words: "When students are 'off task,' our first response should be to ask, 'What's the task?'" (19). He continues:

> Let's be honest: students frequently perceive the tasks they are given as not worth doing—and sometimes with good reason. Worksheets and textbooks and lectures are often hard to justify pedagogically. Even an assignment that could in principle be worthwhile may fail to engage students because its meaning and relevance were never explained, or because students had nothing to say about how it was to be done. (19)

I was drawn to Kohn's approach and insights because, in my own teaching, I work with the same assumption; but I express it in a different way. I use the analogy "If the horse dies . . . dismount!" Sometimes lessons or activities don't work out. Your instructional "horse" dies. *It happens sometimes.* It doesn't matter *why* at the moment. You can reflect later on the problem when you have some time available to make needed revisions. The important thing is to "dismount" and jump on a different horse. This is why it's so essential to have backup plans available, just in case—so you won't get caught with your *plans* down. Try a different activity, or try another approach to the same material or topic. I tell my methods students, "The first time that you find that your horse has died and you don't have any other horses available to ride, and you begin praying for a fire drill . . . that's the moment when you'll consider seriously the value of backup plans."

Classroom management problems occur when teachers are unwilling to dismount a dead horse—to drop a lesson that's not working and try something else. Instead, teachers try such strategies as buying a stronger whip, telling the students to kick the horse harder, or changing riders (see Figure 2–1).

If the Horse Dies, Dismount

Common advice from knowledgeable horse trainers includes the adage "If the horse dies, dismount!" Seems simple enough, yet we don't always follow that advice in the education business. Instead, we often choose from an array of other alternatives, which include:

- Buying a stronger whip.

- Telling the students to kick it harder.

- Changing riders.

- Moving the horse to a new location.

- Riding the horse for longer periods of time.

- Saying things like, "This is the way we've always ridden this horse."

- Appointing a committee to study the horse.

- Arranging to visit other sites where people ride dead horses more efficiently.

- Increasing the standards for riding dead horses.

- Creating a test for measuring our riding ability.

- Complaining about the state of horses these days.

- Blaming the horse's parents. The problem is often in the breeding.

- Passing a resolution declaring "This horse is not dead."

- Harnessing several dead horses together for increased speed.

- Declaring that "No horse is too dead to beat."

- Providing additional funding to increase the horse's performance.

- Forming a quality circle to find uses for dead horses.

Figure 2–1. "If the Horse Dies . . . Dismount!"

There is another strategy that teachers sometimes use when they are confronted with a dead horse and are reluctant to dismount. They resort to using rewards and punishments. But, both of these strategies are equally bad, in Kohn's view. They are both manipulative ways to obtain *temporary* compliance, but what happens when these rewards and punishments are removed? You're back where you started, needing to find other ways to get the students to comply with your rules and requests. In addition, when using rewards and punishments, you, the teacher, are put in the role of enforcer, constantly having to patrol the class to find those who should be rewarded and those others who "colored outside the lines" and should be punished. Not exactly a desirable role or function for *any* teacher.

To avoid having to deal with this problem of compliance—having to find ways to "make the students do what you want them to do"—one can establish a climate of *engagement* instead.

Making Engagement Happen

It might help at this point to distinguish between the two concepts *motivation* and *engagement*. Motivation is another concern often expressed by my methods students: "I want to learn how to motivate students" or "How do you get students motivated to do the work?" Unfortunately, I don't know how to motivate students. Sorry—can't help you there. If students need to be *motivated* to do the work, it suggests that the work may not be worth doing. Is this strategy of motivating students the same thing as trying to find a way to get the students to comply with your directions and demands? If the coursework is worth doing, why would you have to *motivate* the students to do it?

Engagement is different. Engagement happens when students participate actively and enthusiastically in the task at hand without the threat of a grade or the promise of points or a pizza party. Engaging activities do not require students to be motivated first in order to attract their attention and interest and involvement. The characteristics and structure of the activity are in themselves enough to elicit the students' active and immediate participation.

The characteristics I'm referring to above—the ones that make this kind of engagement happen—are the *principles* upon which an interactive classroom is built. These principles are the essential ingredients for any lesson plan, any activity, any project, any time. Structure your activities so that students are performing with language, communicating for real purposes and real audiences, and using their own talk as a means of learning. Infuse these characteristics into your coursework, and engagement will happen. Neglect them, and you'll have something else going—probably something that will require you to motivate the students first and obtain their compliance in order to persuade them to participate.

Constructing a Classroom Community

Providing activities that are challenging, engaging, worthwhile, and fun is certainly a large part of successfully managing the classroom communication environment, but it is also important to build a sense of community. Students need to feel that they are integral parts and respected members of the class, that they *belong* there, that their voices will be heard and their thoughts considered by others.

Such a feeling cannot be developed as long as students remain invisible and unknown to their classmates. I described several community-building activities in my 1994 book, *Activities for an Interactive Classroom*, including the "Warm Fuzzies" (8–13), "Tell Us About . . ." (17–19), "Introduction Speech" (19–20), "Brainstorming in Small Groups" (21–25), "Hidden Figures" (25–28), and the "Writing Notes" exercise (28–29). Run these activities *early in the year* with your students. They are engaging activities that encourage students to work together and value one another's contributions. They also establish the tone or climate for the class, a climate of cooperation and active student participation.

Following are some additional community-building activities.

The Scavenger Hunt

In this activity, students get up out of their seats to talk with their classmates and find those who have done certain things or possess certain traits. It's a way to celebrate students and their accomplishments and to highlight students' individuality.

To prepare for this activity, you will need to design your own version of the Scavenger Hunt sheet (see Figure 2–2). Create and list items suitable for use with your own students. For instance, if you are working with middle school students, you probably will not have an item on your list that says, "Find someone who . . . received a traffic ticket." Since my students live in Florida, I included such items as ". . . went to Disney World recently" and ". . . can name four of the islands in the Florida Keys." You might want to substitute different items of more relevance to your own geographical area.

Hand out copies of your customized Scavenger Hunt sheet to your students with these directions:

> "In a moment, you will get out of your seats and go around the room, trying to find classmates who can put their initials beside these various items. Please sign a maximum

Getting to Know Your Classmates Through an Information Scavenger Hunt

INTRODUCTION: Our class consists of individuals with special talents, interests, and backgrounds. As you move around the room and talk with your classmates, get one signature beside each item. One person can sign no more than two blanks on any sheet.

Find someone who . . .

1. has never had a cavity. _____
2. has lived in a foreign country. _____
3. scored more than 100,000 points on a video arcade game. _____
4. can recite the first line of the Gettysburg Address. _____
5. speaks a foreign language fluently. _____
6. visits Web sites often. _____
7. has won a contest. _____
8. has competed in an athletic event in the past two years. _____
9. went to Disney World recently. _____
10. can name four of the islands in the Florida Keys. _____
11. subscribes to at least two magazines. _____
12. has a celebrity's autograph. _____
13. has had a broken bone. _____
14. has won an award. _____
15. has been to a movie sometime during the past week. _____
16. has an unusual collection or hobby. _____
17. has gone bungee jumping. _____
18. is an only child. _____
19. can play a musical instrument. _____
20. has been written about in a newspaper or magazine. _____
21. read at least two books for pleasure last year. _____
22. has an unusual pet (something other than a cat, dog, or bird). _____
23. is left-handed. _____
24. received a traffic ticket. _____
25. loves chocolate. _____
26. is an artist. _____
27. likes to cook. _____
28. has an e-mail account. _____
29. has ridden the new roller coaster at Busch Gardens. _____
30. knows the principal's first name. _____
31. has a birthday this month. _____
32. knows the names of at least three of the four Teenage Mutant Ninja Turtles. _____

Figure 2–2. An Information Scavenger Hunt

of only *two items* on any one sheet even though you may find that more than two of these items apply to you. That way, people will have to visit many different classmates to get all the items signed."

And you, the teacher, also participate in this activity, signing your students' sheets and going around the room looking for students to sign *your* sheet. After about ten minutes, instruct the students to return to their seats and then begin the next part of this activity:

> "Students, let's go over some of these items and find out who has done some of these things and hear the details. Please understand that your participation is entirely voluntary here. Okay, let's start with item number two: Who has lived in a foreign country? . . . Which country have you lived in?"

Continue in this way, going through the more interesting items, especially the ones that might involve students in telling some stories. For instance, the item ". . . has won a contest" invites the student to give details about which contest he or she entered and what he or she did in order to win it. The item ". . . has an unusual collection or hobby" is sure to elicit some fascinating details. You will often find that students begin asking follow-up questions of their classmates as they listen to these stories of the award that was won last year or the movie seen last week or the book just read.

What is happening here with this sharing of items and stories is that you are "celebrating" students and their accomplishments and other aspects that distinguish them as unique individuals. The students are becoming *visible* and *known* to each other through stories and details.

A community is beginning to form.

The "Wanted" Poster

Creating "Wanted" posters is a lighthearted way for students to play with language and engage in a form of low-risk self-disclosure, too. I use my own "Wanted" poster as a model (see Figure 2–3), reading it aloud and then handing out copies of the poster and the accompanying directions (see Figure 2–4). I instruct students to design their own "Wanted" posters at home, and after about a week, bring the posters into class, share them by reading them aloud, and then display them on the classroom walls. I have used this exercise with both ninth graders and my methods students at the university. Both groups thoroughly enjoyed this activity, and many of my former methods students who have now gained teaching positions are routinely doing the "Wanted" posters with their students during the first month of the school year.

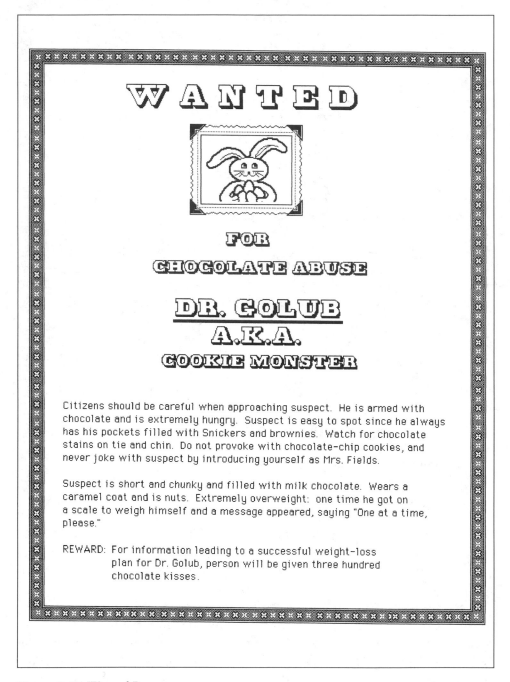

Figure 2–3. Wanted Poster

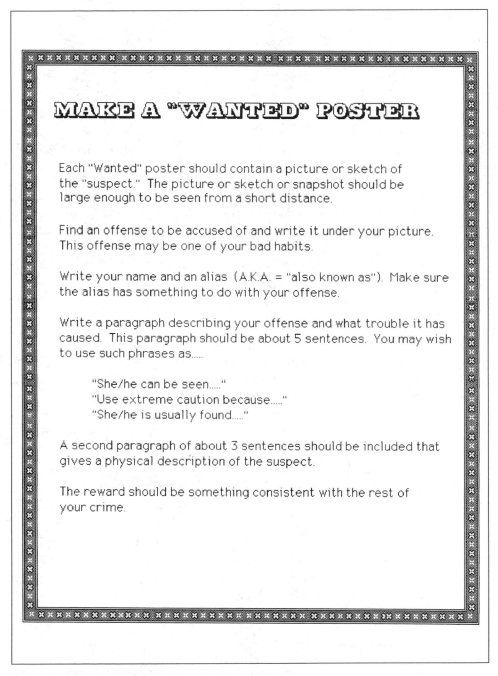

MAKE A "WANTED" POSTER

Each "Wanted" poster should contain a picture or sketch of the "suspect." The picture or sketch or snapshot should be large enough to be seen from a short distance.

Find an offense to be accused of and write it under your picture. This offense may be one of your bad habits.

Write your name and an alias (A.K.A. = "also known as"). Make sure the alias has something to do with your offense.

Write a paragraph describing your offense and what trouble it has caused. This paragraph should be about 5 sentences. You may wish to use such phrases as.....

> "She/he can be seen....."
> "Use extreme caution because....."
> "She/he is usually found....."

A second paragraph of about 3 sentences should be included that gives a physical description of the suspect.

The reward should be something consistent with the rest of your crime.

Figure 2–4. Directions for Making a "Wanted" Poster

A Writer's Profile

Either at the beginning of the school year or the beginning of a writing unit, use the "Writer's Profile" exercise as a means of engaging the students in reflection on their writing habits and style. It also serves to establish a sense of community as students come to realize that they are not alone in their concerns about various aspects of their writing abilities.

Hand out copies of the "Writer's Profile" assignment (see Figure 2–5). Read the background information and instructions and direct students to write a profile of themselves *as a writer.* Tell your students:

> "The questions listed on the sheet are meant to serve merely as suggestions for what you might write about. You do not have to answer each question; in fact, some of you may devote most of your paper to responding to only two or three questions. That's fine. Others may concentrate on four or five of these questions and ignore the rest. That's fine, too. But, responding to *any* of these questions will provide important insights—for you and me—about your writing habits, style, and concerns. That's important information for *both* of us to have."

After students have completed a draft of their essays, they should assemble in small groups of four or five students each and share their papers. Students can either read their papers aloud to the classmates in their group, or they can pass the papers around the circle. They should look for similarities between all of the papers in their group. What writing habits and concerns are mentioned most often in the papers? Do many of the students report that they tend to wait until the last day to complete an assignment? Do they find that the hardest part of writing a paper is coming up with the first sentence?

Once students have finished reading all the papers in their groups and have had an opportunity to create a list of the similarities they found, invite representatives from each group to report their findings. This exercise has a community-building effect because it lets students see that they are not alone in their worries about writing. They learn that many of their classmates also have trouble with this or that aspect of writing; that there are others who enjoy writing fantasy, too; that several others also hate it when the teacher assigns the topic and tells them how they must write the paper. This is important information for the students, and it will help establish a feeling of "connectedness" between classmates.

The "Something Important" Speech

I have already described this "Something Important" speech exercise in my *Activities* (1994) book, but because it is such an effective element in a community-building

---

A Writer's Profile

INTRODUCTION: If you were asked to give a *profile* of yourself *as a student,* you would probably write about the kinds of classes you like and don't like; the grades you've earned; your study habits (where, when, and how you tend to study best); a description of something you've read or done or heard in class; and perhaps your future plans for college. Writing about these kinds of topics would indeed allow your reader to come to know you *as a student.*

Relax! I'm *not* going to ask you to write about how you see yourself as a student. *Instead,* I am asking you to give me a profile of yourself *as a writer.* Since you have probably done a fair amount of writing in school, I am assuming that you know something already about how *you* write. Tell me what you know.

DIRECTIONS: In a well-organized, clear, Insightful composition, describe yourself *as a writer.* You might consider writing about some of the following ideas, but please do not feel pressured to deal with all of these topics. They are merely suggestions to get you started.

- How do you write? (Do you draft the whole paper at once? do sections at a time? wait until the night before the paper is due?) Where and when do you write best?

- What is the hardest part of the writing process for you? (Is it the drafting? the editing? coming up with your first sentence? or what?) What is the easiest part?

- Do you generally like what you have written? Or do you find that you are rarely satisfied with your work? How can you tell when you have written something good?

- What kinds of writing do you like to do most (narrative, descriptive, creative, persuasive, etc.; stories, poems, essays, letters, journals, etc.)? What do you like the least?

- What have you learned from your past English classes that has helped you most with your writing? (Don't be afraid to say "Nothing." It happens sometimes.)

- What else can you say about yourself as a writer?

Figure 2–5. A Writer's Profile

effort, I want to go over it again, this time adding comments and providing a context for the strategy. This powerful exercise makes the students "real" to one another. It will establish a bond between classmates that will last throughout the semester. I have conducted this activity with both junior and senior high school students while teaching in Seattle, and now I conduct it with my methods students each semester.

This activity should be almost the last one you run in your series of community-building strategies. You've completed the Scavenger Hunt, the "Wanted" poster, and perhaps a few other introductory exercises, too (see also the section on brainstorming activities in Chapter 4, (pages 54–79). You might also consider engaging your students in some of the listening activities described in the next chapter before you do the "Something Important" speech. The listening exercises get students up out of their seats and working with one another, and the exercises also give a real interactive feeling to the class.

Only after you have completed several of these kinds of activities should you introduce this final and powerful strategy. Here is how I described it in the *Activities* book:

> Here is another opportunity to enable students to learn more about their classmates and get to know each other well. Ask students to bring something to class tomorrow that is *important* to them. "Don't bring in Aunt Minnie's $7,000 stamp collection; that's not what I'm talking about. Simply bring in an object—a stuffed animal, a ring, a letter, a picture—that, for some reason, is very important to you." Sometimes students will bring in a picture of their pet dog or their best friend; others might bring in a baseball glove to *represent* the sport itself that is important.
>
> The next day when students bring these objects to class, ask for a volunteer to come to the front of the room and say a few words about why their object is important to them. Then the class should be allowed to ask follow-up questions. The next volunteer gives his or her speech, and so it goes until all have had a chance to talk in front of the class. You should find that each speech lasts from 1–3 minutes. No need for the students to prepare their talk in advance. A strange thing happens when students bring in something that is genuinely important to them: *the words flow*. The students obviously know their subject well and have something to say about it. A reticent speaker will be encouraged to say more and provide details by the follow-up questions from his or her classmates. Students like this exercise because they are encouraged to share something that has become a part of themselves with a friendly, appreciative audience. Often the student's talk ends with a spontaneous, sincere round of applause for the speaker. (1994, 20–21)

You, the teacher, should be the first one to present your "Something Important" speech. Since this exercise involves a fair amount of self-disclosure, you will show that you are willing to take the same risk that you are asking of your students. In addition, it allows you to model the nature and length of the presentation.

This activity is a powerful one because students—and you—are sharing something of themselves. Many presentations will be accompanied by tears, others by appreciative laughter, but all will be felt emotionally.

What is happening through these presentations is that the students are becoming "real" to one another. After all students have spoken, I explain this concept to the class by introducing and describing the wonderful children's story *The Velveteen Rabbit* (1983) by Margery Williams, and I read aloud the excerpt about "What Is Real?":

The Skin Horse had lived longer in the nursery than any of the others. He was so old that his brown coat was bald in patches and showed the seams underneath, and most of the hairs in his tail had been pulled out to string bead necklaces. He was wise, for he had seen a long succession of mechanical toys arrive to boast and swagger, and by-and-by break their mainsprings and pass away, and he knew that they were only toys, and would never turn into anything else. For nursery magic is very strange and wonderful, and only those playthings that are old and wise and experienced like the Skin Horse understand all about it.

"What is REAL?" asked the Rabbit one day, when they were lying side by side near the nursery fender, before Nana came to tidy the room. "Does it mean having things that buzz inside you and a stick-out handle?"

"Real isn't how you are made," said the Skin Horse. "It's a thing that happens to you. When a child loves you for a long, long time, not just to play with, but REALLY loves you, then you become Real."

"Does it hurt?" asked the Rabbit.

"Sometimes," said the Skin Horse, for he was always truthful. "When you are Real you don't mind being hurt."

"Does it happen all at once, like being wound up," he asked, "or bit by bit?"

"It doesn't happen all at once," said the Skin Horse. "You become. It takes a long time. That's why it doesn't often happen to people who break easily, or have sharp edges, or who have to be carefully kept. Generally, by the time you are Real, most of your hair has been loved off, and your eyes drop out and you get loose in the joints and very shabby. But these things don't matter at all, because once you are Real you can't be ugly, except to people who don't understand."

I conclude the activity with this explanation:

"Students, look around the room at your classmates. What do you see? Can you see the stories? Wonderful, lovely stories. Stories of accomplishments and friendships and caring and loss and pride. Through your presentations, you have become 'Real' to one another. You look at your classmates now and see other caring, feeling persons who are just like you."

This activity, used in combination with the other strategies described earlier, works well to create a powerful and lasting sense of community in the classroom.

Conclusion

A teacher is "a coordinator of a communication environment," and one can coordinate this environment successfully by designing engaging activities and creating a sense of community. Students should not only be enthusiastic about riding the instructional horses you bring into the classroom, but they should also come to enjoy the company of their fellow riders.

Notes

1. L. E. Sarbaugh, 1979, *Teaching Speech Communication* (Columbus, OH: Charles E. Merrill), 9.
2. A. Kohn, 1996, *Beyond Discipline: From Compliance to Community* (Alexandria, VA: Association for Supervision and Curriculum Development), 10.

Works Cited

Golub, J. N. 1994. *Activities for an Interactive Classroom.* Urbana, IL: National Council of Teachers of English.

Kohn, A. 1996. *Beyond Discipline: From Compliance to Community.* Alexandria, VA: Association for Supervision and Curriculum Development.

Williams, M. 1983. *The Velveteen Rabbit or How Toys Become Real.* Simon & Schuster Books for Young Readers.

3

Developing Students' Speaking and Listening Skills

If we are serious about improving our students' performance with language, then we must focus on students' oral communication skills as well as on their writing and reading abilities. Students perform with language just as much when they speak and listen as when they write and read, and they engage in oral communication constantly. Much of students' learning, moreover, occurs through their use of oral communication strategies as they work to construct and comprehend meanings and understand what they hear and read. It makes sense, then, to focus their attention on the competencies involved—make these invisible skills visible—and design activities and instructional strategies that will help students "gain a measure of control"[1] over these skills.

Oral communication is a process involving meaning making just as much as reading and writing are meaning-making processes. People's oral communication behavior involves making sense of what they hear, interpreting not only the words used, but the speaker's tone and other nonverbal cues. There's a *relationship* aspect to oral communication, too, that affects how one shapes his or her messages. One's communication behavior is influenced by his or her perception of his or her relationship to the audience. It's a *transaction* involving as much self-definition as it does self-disclosure. It's a complicated process.

Students need help and practice to expand their repertoire of appropriate oral communication skills in order to participate successfully in these transactions. They need to learn to select appropriately from the range of skills that are available to them, reflect on their developing oral communication competence, and evaluate the success of their efforts to communicate clearly and effectively.

The purpose of the activities described in this chapter is to make the invisible oral communication skills visible to the students—to make the students aware of what skills are involved in effective speaking and listening—and then engage the students in activities that allow them to practice or rehearse these skills with their classmates.

Developing Listening Ability

Some of the most engaging ways to develop students' listening skills come from the field of creative drama. I have listed a couple of creative drama texts at the end of this chapter, and I recommend them to you as excellent resources for pertinent and valuable activities.

The following activities are ones that I use to develop students' ability to *concentrate*. Concentration is a basic element involved in effective listening, and I want students to be aware of the importance of this element and to rehearse and improve their own concentration skills. I usually conduct these activities early in the semester because they also serve to help build a sense of community. They require that students get up and out of their seats and participate actively with their classmates.

Simultaneous Interviews[2]

For all of the following activities, you will first need to ask for student volunteers to demonstrate the exercise in front of the class. In this way, students will learn quickly about the structure and procedure involved. After the demonstration, you can have all the students find partners and do the exercise themselves. It is extremely important that for the demonstrations, you ask for *volunteers*. Don't simply choose the students yourself. If you do so, the students participating in the demonstration might feel intimidated or embarrassed, and these are two feelings that don't belong in *any* classroom.

For this first activity, you will need three student volunteers to come up to the front of the class. Arrange the students as shown in Figure 3–1. Students B and C are going to interview student A. This interview should consist of more in-depth questions than simply "What's your favorite color?" or "What's your favorite food?" B and C might ask student A about how his or her classes are going, what he or she plans to do next summer, or about a field trip taken recently. Anything like that should get A talking at length.

But here's the hard part, the part that requires concentration: students B and C will be conducting their interviews *simultaneously* with student A, and A must

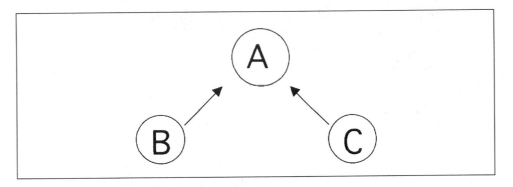

Figure 3–1. Arrangement of Students for Simultaneous Interviews

keep up both conversations. B and C also have a difficult task: each has to tune out the other interviewer, focusing solely on his or her own conversation with student A.

Explain the procedure to the student volunteers and the class, and then direct the volunteers to begin. Because students B and C—the interviewers—are probably very polite students, they are likely to proceed like this: B will ask a question first and then wait for C to ask a question, and then it will be B's turn again and . . . No, you need to point out during the demonstration that that's not how it's done. B and C should begin talking and asking questions of A *immediately* and *continuously*, trying to ignore the other interview that is going on at the same time.

Allow the demonstration to proceed for a few minutes, just long enough for the class to get the idea of how it works and what it sounds like. Then stop the demonstration and direct all students to arrange themselves in groups of three for this activity.

Start all groups working at the same time; allow the interviews to go on for a few minutes; then stop the groups and instruct the students to begin again, this time with A and C interviewing person B. After a few minutes more, stop the groups again and announce that for the third round, person C will be interviewed.

This activity makes the concept of concentration *visible* to the students by placing them in a situation where they actually have to concentrate. It's another way to help students understand what concentration is and what it feels like when one is doing it. Awareness is the beginning of change, and this first exercise makes students aware of this important listening skill.

You might conduct this exercise two or three more times during the week, each time directing students to work with different classmates in their group. In this way, students will have an opportunity to interact with many different people, and a sense of community will emerge and become another benefit of using this strategy.

Simultaneous Monologues[3]

Ask for two volunteers to come to the front of the class to demonstrate this activity. Arrange the two students so that they are facing each other, as shown in Figure 3–2.

Tell students A and B that they need to think of a story to tell each other. This story should not be a fictional tale or a summary of a book they have read, but a recounting of a personal experience: a trip they took one summer; a class at school they found particularly interesting and helpful; a project they are working on at home or in the community—anything like that. This story should provide them with enough content for a monologue lasting at least thirty seconds.

When both students indicate that they have the story in mind that they will tell, give the further directions that they should begin simultaneously telling their stories to each other. While doing so, they must tune out their partner and his or her story, concentrating instead on delivering their own monologue. Not too difficult to do if one simply stares at the floor while speaking; but in this case, students A and B must maintain eye contact throughout the exercise.

This is a difficult exercise because it is relatively easy to lose one's concentration and focus instead on the story being told by one's partner. And the constant eye contact during this activity makes it especially challenging. At the conclusion of the demonstration, direct all students in the class to find a partner and begin when they and their partner agree that they have both thought of a story to tell.

You might conduct this exercise two or three times, each time directing students to find a new partner. Again, students are up and out of their seats, interacting with classmates and building a classroom community. This exercise could also serve as a good prewriting activity for a unit on narrative writing in general or a personal experience essay.

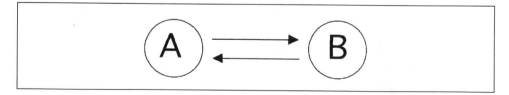

Figure 3–2. Arrangement of Students for Simultaneous Monologues

The King and His Servants[4]

Ask for five student volunteers to come to the front of the room and line up in a row facing the class. The directions for this activity begin with this story:

"Once upon a time, there was a mythical king in a mythical land who loved to hear stories. Just couldn't get enough of them. That was the good news! The bad news is that he was a very cruel king, so whenever he wanted to hear a story, he would summon his servants and line them up in a row . . . well, sort of like this . . . [pointing to the row of student volunteers] . . . and point to one of the servants suddenly, growling, 'Tell me a story!' And that servant would have to start telling a tale instantly . . . or else!

"If the king should get tired of hearing from that particular servant, he would suddenly point to another servant, and that hapless soul would have to pick up the story exactly where the first servant left off, even if it were in the middle of a word or a sentence. So this is how the king would get to hear all these wonderful stories—by pointing first to one servant and then to another—and these stories could go on in this way for hours and hours.

"Here, let me show you how it works: [Turning to the student volunteers] 'Hello, Servants!' When I point to you, begin telling me a story. The rest of you should watch carefully, because if I should point to you later, you must pick up the story immediately and continue the narration."

Conduct the demonstration, and when it is finished, direct all students to assemble in groups of five or six students each. Each group should appoint a "king" or "queen" who will do the pointing and thus determine which "servant" speaks at what time.

"Tell Us About . . ."

The first three activities in this chapter have all focused on developing students' concentration skill, a basic skill involved in effective listening. This fourth activity, however, is designed to develop three other listening skills simultaneously. These skills are

- focusing on the speaker,
- drawing out the speaker through questions, and
- listening without judging.

This exercise is a powerful community-building activity as well as an effective listening strategy. I first described it in my 1994 book, *Activities for an Interactive*

Classroom, but, because of its importance and relevance to this series of other listening activities, I thought it should be reprinted here for easy reference:

Have students select a partner for this activity. Distribute to each student a copy of the "Tell Us About . . ." sheet that lists possible topics for this exercise [see Figure 3–3]. Explain that one person in each pair will select a topic from this sheet and begin talking about it to his or her partner. While the person is talking, the partner will practice these three listening skills: (1) Focusing, (2) Drawing the person out through questions, and (3) Listening without judging.

(*Note:* Two students, Steve and Odalys, have kindly volunteered to serve as models for this exercise. Odalys agreed to select a topic from the sheet and begin talking first, so Steve will be practicing the listening skills.) Describe to the students how these skills are applied in the activity:

Focusing—While Odalys is talking about her subject, Steve will keep the focus of attention on *her.* The focus is lost if, for instance, Odalys says at one point: "I took a trip to New York last summer," and Steve immediately replies, "Oh, I went there once, too! Let me tell you about it!" Keep the focus on the person who is speaking.

Drawing the person out through questions—As Odalys talks, Steve will occasionally ask her questions that he may have about some aspect of her subject. These questions will show Odalys that Steve has indeed been listening to her (How can you ask an appropriate question about something if you haven't really been listening to the speaker?) and that he is interested in what she is saying and wants to know more. So Steve is going to have to listen carefully as Odalys talks. Perhaps he will hear something that is not clear to him, or he might find that he wants additional details about something particularly interesting. In either case, Steve will ask questions and let Odalys know in this way that he is following her talk and is sincerely interested in what she has to say.

Listening without judging—This is the most difficult skill to master. Imagine Odalys telling about a time when she skipped class to go downtown with some friends, and Steve replies, "Well, THAT was a dumb thing to do!" Steve is expressing a "judgment" of Odalys and her actions, and the first time he does that is the *last* time that Odalys will tell him *anything.* Listen without judging, without expressing either approval or disapproval. Simply listen to learn, and ask questions to draw the person out and invite him or her to say more. But don't evaluate what you hear.

After explaining the three skills, direct the pairs of students to begin the exercise: one student in each pair talks about a topic on the sheet while his or her partner listens, practicing the three listening skills. After 15–20 minutes have passed, instruct the students to "switch": now the partner selects a topic, and the student who *had* been talking gets a chance to practice the listening skills.

Tell Us About . . .

How you spend your free time on weekends.

Something you can do now that you couldn't do a year ago.

How you helped someone once.

What you look for in choosing a friend.

Something you are proud of that you have written, drawn, or made.

Something good that has happened as a result of a choice you made.

Something important that you are planning to do.

Whether you prefer to make choices yourself or have others make choices for you.

Something you are proud of that you have worked hard for.

Something good you have done that not many people know about.

A difficult choice you made recently.

Something you did that took courage to do.

Something important you decided in which you made the choice all by yourself.

Something difficult that you learned that you are proud of.

Who you go to for advice when making important or difficult decisions.

Something that you have done before that you would do differently today.

A choice you made that did not work out the way you had hoped.

A change you would like to make in yourself.

Something about a choice you made that turned out well.

A choice you had to make between two things you wanted very much.

Figure 3–3. Sample Topics for the "Tell Us About . . ." Exercise

At the end of this activity, ask students for their reactions. Did they feel as if their partner were really listening? How did it feel to have someone really listen this closely, asking appropriate questions, and not "judging"?

Repeating this exercise during a few succeeding days and directing students to work with a different partner each time will give them an opportunity to meet and talk with new classmates. Students will have gained an awareness of what is involved in *really* listening. The hard work begins with practicing those skills regularly and frequently throughout the class. (17–19)

At the conclusion of the "Tell Us About . . ." exercise and after all the concentration activities have been run, it would be a good time to introduce the "Something Important" speech (see Chapter 2, pages 24–26). Students will have had several opportunities to meet and work with different classmates and practice effective interpersonal communication skills. Now it's time for them to become "Real."

Playing with Tongue Twisters

It's also time to begin working on the students' *articulation,* a basic skill in speaking. This is the ability to pronounce words clearly and correctly, and it is a most important skill for the students to master. Whether working in a small-group setting or participating in an oral presentation in front of the whole class, students need to develop the habit of speaking clearly, and this activity can help.

We're going to play with tongue twisters here, a fun, engaging way to enable students to practice and improve their articulation skills. The first step is to hand out a list of several tongue twisters (see Figure 3–4) and tell the students to find a partner and practice reading these tongue twisters aloud.

Explain to them:

"Students, the idea is to read them as fast as you can without 'stumbling' over the words. It doesn't do any good for you to read them at lightning speed if no one can understand the words you're saying. You might practice these tongue twisters by having your partner read one aloud, then you read one, and continue going back and forth until you have both practiced all of them."

Allow ten to fifteen minutes for this practice to go on, and then call the class back together:

"Students, at this time I invite volunteers, one at a time, to go to the front of the room and read any one of these tongue twisters aloud. In this way, I can work with you on your voice volume and articulation skill."

Tongue Twisters

1. A big black dog bit a big black bear.
2. Two tall boys bought two toy boats.
3. Face the fancy vase and find the fine vine, Vinnie.
4. Matt's satin hat had saddened Dad, hadn't it?
5. Big black pigs bickered blatantly by Papa's big pigpen, Ben.
6. Billy Button's buttered biscuit was buttered by Betsy Biddle.
7. Twenty-two little tots with twenty-two little metal bottles.
8. Lila and Lula liked light classical melodies.
9. So we say, "Still the sinking steamer sunk."
10. Children chasing chickens stop to search and reach for peaches.
11. The gentle general had the courage to arrange for a college pageant.
12. He looked for the cuckoo clock that tick-tocked for the cat and six kittens.
13. The ragged beggar giggled at the big goose egg on the green grass.
14. National Shropshire Sheep Association.
15. He sawed six long, slim, sleek, slender saplings.
16. Theophilus Thistle, the successful thistle sifter, thrust three thousand thistles through the thick of his thumb.
17. "Are you copper-bottoming them, my man?" "No, I'm aluminuming 'em, Mum."
18. Five and fifty fairies frolicking with forty fluttering fireflies.
19. Tie twine to the tree twigs.
20. Cross crossings cautiously.
21. The sixth sheik's sixth sheep's sick.
22. Lemon liniment.
23. Six thick thistle sticks.
24. Strange strategic statistics.
25. Double bubble gum bubbles double.
26. Sixty-six sick chicks.
27. The sun shines on the shop signs.
28. Eat fresh fried fish free at the fish fry.
29. Much whirling water makes the mill wheel work well.
30. Odd birds always gobble green almonds in the autumn.
31. She makes a proper cup of coffee in a copper coffee pot.
32. Shave a cedar shingle thin.
33. Sinful Caesar sipped his snifter, seized his knees, and sneezed.
34. Would Wheeler woo Wanda if Woody snoozed woozily?
35. Two teamsters tried to steal twenty-two keys.
36. Fill the sieve with thistles; then sift the thistles through the sieve.
37. Six slim, sleek saplings.
38. Better buy bigger rubber baby-buggy bumpers.

Figure 3–4. Tongue Twisters

You should find that students will volunteer readily for this activity, a low-risk opportunity to get up and speak in front of the class. This is good preparation for any speeches or other oral presentations that might occur later in the semester. After all volunteers have come up and read their tongue twisters, you might have the students get together with different partners this time for another round of practice.

The next step in this activity involves the students in writing their own tongue twisters. I point out some prominent characteristics of the tongue twisters they practiced with to get them started in the right direction:

> Notice that all these tongue twisters are silly, nonsensical sentences. And that's what your own tongue twisters should be like, too—the sillier, the better. Notice, also, that each tongue twister plays with a certain *sound*. So here you have thirty-eight examples of different sounds that you can play with. Let's write our own tongue twisters, and then when everyone is finished, we'll go around the room and hear them all.

Fair warning: Do not allow students to use a classmate's name in their tongue twisters . . . even if the classmate gives permission for his or her name to be used. It just doesn't work out well. Feelings will get hurt, and the class climate will suffer.

When all students have finished writing their tongue twisters, ask for a volunteer to read first and then proceed from that student around the room, hearing from everyone else. Be sure to tell students, "If, for some reason, you don't wish to read your tongue twister, simply say 'Pass!' when your turn comes, and we'll just go on to the next student." It is important to allow students to pass if they want. It happens, sometimes, that a student doesn't want to contribute, and pressure to speak should not be applied.

After all students have read their tongue twisters, you might pass out index cards and invite students to write their sentences on the cards. Collect the cards; type up the tongue twisters, along with the author's name, on a sheet; and hand out copies of the sheet to students the next day. In this way, students will have a permanent, published record of their contributions.

Here are some tongue twisters that my students have created in years past. You should expect to receive similarly silly sentences from your own crafty classes (Say that last sentence five times quickly!):

- Take time to twist and tangle your words in tricky, trying tongue twisters.
- Shy sheep sleep in silver ships.
- He ripped a wrench from the wrestling ring and wrote a rousing rosy bruise on the beastly behemoth.
- She should shop nonstop.
- Witty Willy whipped the wizard who wore white whistles.

- Choosy chipmunks chopped their chestnuts, chewing cheerfully with chunky cheeks.
- Franny Friday followed four fraggling frogs.
- Pretty people pick practical parts in plays.
- See Sam swim sideways.

Playing with these tongue twisters, by the way, is an excellent strategy to communicate the meaning of the poetic term *alliteration*. Your students are not likely to forget what the term means after this series of activities.

Giving Directions Clearly

Another basic skill is the ability to give directions clearly, and the following sequence of engaging activities gives students the opportunity to improve this skill in both oral and written modes.

Airport[5]

This first activity allows students to assess how well they give directions currently before they receive instruction and information designed to improve their skill. A description of this activity is provided by Samuel Elkind in his book *Improvisation Handbook* (1975). First read the description, and then I will suggest a variation you might try also:

> Two rows of chairs are lined up to suggest the landing approach to an airport runway. One player is chosen to be the pilot, another to function as the control tower. The airport is engulfed by fog, and the pilot is unfamiliar with the airport. Obstacles such as books, clothing, and blackboard erasers are placed in the approach. The pilot is blindfolded. As he stands at the end of the approach, you might turn him slowly around several times to disorient him, or you might rearrange the obstacles after he has been blindfolded. The pilot then begins his approach. The control tower "talks" him through, around, and/or over the obstacles. If the pilot touches an obstacle, his plane crashes. The game is over when the pilot crashes or lands successfully, and a new pilot and control tower take over. (13)

I prepare for this activity by lining up two rows of chairs or student desks as suggested in the above description. Then I litter the space between the two rows with a wastebasket and piles of books and whatever else I can find handy. I ask for two volunteers to demonstrate this activity. Let's imagine that Theoni and Jennifer come forward for this purpose. After positioning Jennifer at one end of the "runway," I tell her to close her eyes. She will be the "pilot." Theoni then begins to give instructions to Jennifer to guide her through the runway.

Here's the variation: As soon as Jennifer begins moving down the runway, going from one end to the other, I ask for two more volunteers and have that team of one pilot and one control tower start at the other end of the runway. This means that somewhere near the center of the runway, the two pilots will have to maneuver, with the help of their respective control towers, to avoid "crashing into" each other. I keep on asking for additional volunteer teams until I fill the runway with about eight pilots. Four pilots are moving one way down the runway, and four others are heading in the opposite direction. At this point, the control towers begin talking with each other: "Okay, I'll move my pilot to the left here so your pilot can get through this space . . ." Makes for quite a scene in the classroom!

At the conclusion of the activity, ask students to reflect on such questions as

- What was the most difficult aspect of this exercise?
- Which directions gave you the most trouble?
- For the pilots: What directions did you find confusing?
- For the control towers: If you were to do this again, what would you do differently?

One-Way Versus Two-Way Communication[6]

The next exercise is an old one, but it fits in well with this sequence of activities and provides important information and insights for students. You are going to make visible to the students the characteristics of and differences between one-way and two-way communication.

For the first part of the exercise, Pat, a student volunteer, will attempt to communicate a particular design (see Figure 3–5) to her classmates, who will try to draw the design according to Pat's directions. The communication, however, must be done in a one-way format: Classmates cannot ask questions, seek clarification of directions, or request that any directions be repeated. Nor should the classmates express any nonverbal communication through grunts or groans or other physical signs of frustration. Pat must simply give the directions as best she can and then sit down. You, the teacher, should keep track of the amount of time it takes for Pat to finish giving all the directions. You will need this information later.

As soon as Pat finishes with her directions, ask the following questions of the class, using the accompanying chart to record the responses (see Figure 3–6):

"Students, before I show you the design that Pat was trying to describe to you, I want to know how many of you think you got *all four rectangles* placed correctly on your paper. I'm not concerned about the *size* of the rectangles; just the *position* of the rectangles in relationship to one another."

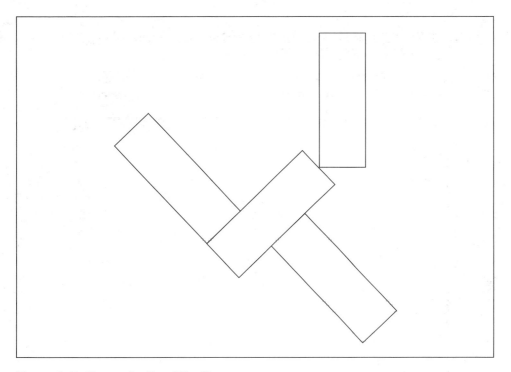

Figure 3–5. Design for One-Way Communication

Record the number of responses in the top left-hand box under Column A on the chart. Ask how many students think they drew three of the four rectangles correctly; then two rectangles; etc. Fill in the boxes under Column A with this information.

Now ask Pat to draw the design on the blackboard or overhead projector. Then ask how many students *did* draw all four rectangles correctly; three of the four rectangles; etc. Fill in Column B on the chart with the numbers of these responses.

At this point, you have completed the demonstration of one-way communication. Save any reflective discussion until after the second half of this activity. At that time, you and your students will be able to see the differences between one-way and two-way communication.

A different student volunteer—Joan this time—will now attempt to describe a second design to her classmates (see Figure 3–7). This time, however, the students may ask all the questions they want. They can ask Joan to repeat a step or to clarify any part of the given directions. Once again, keep track of the amount of time it takes for Joan to communicate all the directions, and then fill in Columns C and D as before with students' responses to this second drawing.

One-Way Communication Versus Two-Way Communication

	Estimate Column A	Actual Column B	Estimate Column C	Actual Column D
4				
3				
2				
1				
0				

Figure 3–6. Chart for "One-Way Versus Two-Way Communication" Exercise

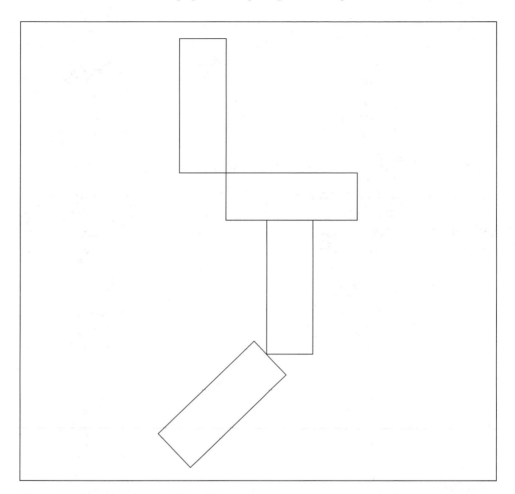

Figure 3–7. Design for Two-Way Communication

A whole-class discussion of students' reactions to this activity should follow the completion of the second drawing and the filling in of the "One-Way Versus Two-Way Communication" chart. Insights that are likely to emerge from this discussion include these points:

- It takes much longer to complete the two-way communication of directions than the one-way format because of the opportunity for the audience to ask questions and correct misperceptions, clarify directions, and obtain additional details. But the two-way communication format also results in much more accurate results.

- One-way communication is more frustrating for the audience than for the speaker. The audience is frustrated that it cannot get the clarification and elaboration it needs to complete the task well.
- Two-way communication is more frustrating for the speaker because of all the audience's questions and feedback indicating that the speaker's directions are too vague or incomplete despite his or her best attempts to communicate clearly.

The "Giving Directions Clearly" Writing Activity

Rehearsal The last activity provided some insight into the difficulties involved in giving directions, but only two students had the opportunity to actually practice this skill while the rest of the class simply tried to comprehend the directions given. In this exercise, *all* students practice both giving and following directions. I have adapted this activity from an instructional strategy described by T. J. Ray in the NCTE volume *Writing Exercises from* Exercise Exchange (1976). Begin by saying:

> "Students, please find a partner for this next activity. One of you should move to a seat on one side of the room and your partner should sit in a seat on the other side. You do not have to be directly opposite each other, but everyone on this side of the room should have a partner seated somewhere on that side. You will need sheets of paper and something to write with for this exercise."

After students have arranged themselves for this exercise, hand out copies of the first four designs (see Figure 3–8) to all the students seated on one side of the room and copies of the last four designs (see Figure 3–9) to the students' partners seated on the opposite side. Then continue:

> "Students, your task is to select one of the four designs on the sheet just given to you and begin writing directions for how to draw that design. At any time, you can hand me your directions and I will give them to your partner, who will try to follow your directions and reproduce your design. You and your partner each have four different designs, so you will both be writing your own directions and trying to follow your partner's directions.
>
> "In writing your instructions, you may choose to write the first two steps only and then have your partner try to follow those directions before you continue writing. Or you can write out all the directions before you send them to your partner. The choice is yours. You can send messages back and forth as many times as you want, and I will serve as the messenger for your notes and directions. In your notes to your partner, feel free to ask questions, seeking clarification and elaboration of the instructions that your partner has written for you.
>
> "You have completed this exercise when both you and your partner have drawn each other's design accurately."

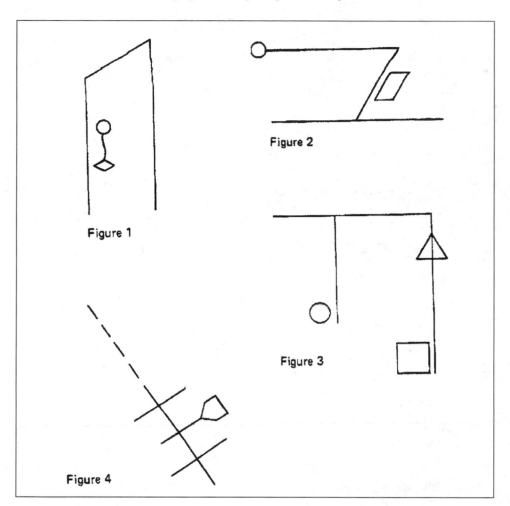

Figure 1

Figure 2

Figure 3

Figure 4

Figure 3–8. "Giving Directions Clearly" Designs #1–4

This activity will take about twenty to thirty minutes to complete, and students will experience firsthand just how difficult it is to communicate directions clearly. But, they will also discover some creative ways to *clarify* their directions—using comparisons and word-pictures, for instance, to communicate their ideas ("It looks like a slanted door." "The rectangle has a shape on top that looks like a lampshade." "Draw a circle about as big as a nickel.").

Students who finish early, meaning both partners have successfully drawn each other's design, should be encouraged to select a second design on the sheet and try writing the directions for that one, too.

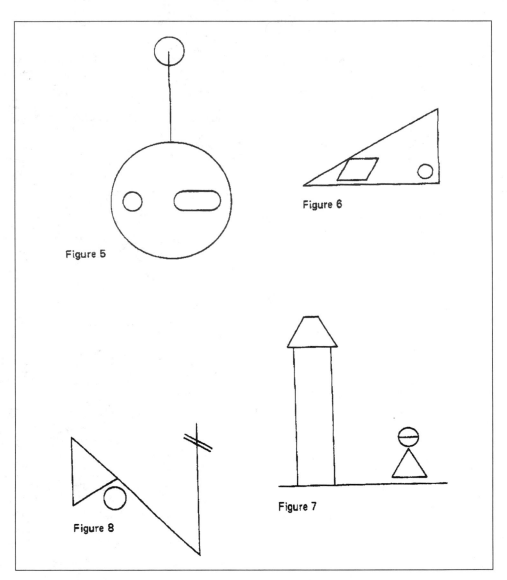

Figure 3–9. "Giving Directions Clearly" Designs #5–8

A whole-class discussion after the completion of the activity might focus on such questions as (1) What parts of your design gave you the most trouble as you tried to write clear directions? (2) What did you find most difficult or confusing about your partner's directions? (3) What have you learned about ways to communicate directions clearly and accurately?

Performance The three previous activities in this unit on giving directions clearly have all been "rehearsals," providing students with low-risk opportunities to assess their current level of skill, gain pertinent information and insights, and practice and improve their ability to write clear and complete directions.

This next activity, however, is a "performance," requiring that students exhibit a competent demonstration of this skill. It challenges students to create a more detailed, extensive set of directions, but with the opportunity once again to get helpful feedback from a real audience. Explain to the class:

> "Students, this time you're going to create your *own* design, using lines, circles, triangles, or any other figures you wish to include. Draw your design and then write the directions that will enable someone else to reproduce your design accurately and completely.
>
> "After you have written a rough draft of your directions, try them out on your classmates. Give your directions to other students in the class and have them try to follow your instructions. Find out where your directions are too vague, confusing, or incomplete. Then revise your directions to make them clearer and easier to follow and try them out again with a different classmate.
>
> "When you think that your directions are both complete and accurate, make a 'final copy.' You will hand in two separate sheets. On one sheet will be a drawing of your design with the word ORIGINAL at the top. Your directions will be written on the other sheet.
>
> "I will give your directions to students in another class, and they will attempt to follow your instructions as best they can. Their drawing will come back with the word COPY at the top. I will compare your original and their copy. If the two are similar, you will have earned an A for this assignment. But, if there are some major differences, it means that your directions still need some more clarification or elaboration. In that case, you will be given another opportunity to make the necessary revisions, and we'll send out your 'new and improved' directions again for another trial.
>
> "Everyone will earn an A for this assignment. How many trials and revisions it will take you to *get* that A is up to you."

Through the above series of activities, students first practice and improve their skills in giving directions clearly and then demonstrate their competence in a final performance. Notice that the performance above requires students to exhibit their new and improved skills in the written mode only. But there is also the matter of learning to give directions clearly in the *oral* mode, and it, too, deserves our attention. For that, we turn to the Demonstration Talk.

The Demonstration Talk

The Demonstration Talk is a basic speech activity that can serve well as a culminating performance for this unit designed to improve students' speaking and listening skills. All of the previous activities have helped to serve as rehearsals for this final performance:

- The community-building activities and concentration exercises prepared the students to be a courteous, supportive audience for their classmates' speeches;
- the work with tongue twisters served to improve students' public-speaking voices and build confidence as the students took turns getting up in front of their classmates; and
- the "Giving Directions Clearly" activities provided students with needed practice and important information and insights that they can use in their preparation and presentation of this speech.

Conducting the Demonstration Talk at this time has some additional advantages:

- It serves as a complement to the previous activity on writing directions, developing students' ability to give directions clearly through *oral communication*.
- Unlike other, more formal speeches, students are using more than just their voices here: their hands are busy, and they are often moving around during their demonstrations. Thus, students' feelings of self-consciousness are minimized during this particular talk.
- The Demonstration Talk, similar to the "Something Important" speech, celebrates students and their special traits and abilities. Students' demonstrations often exhibit a special talent or accomplishment.

Directions to the Students

"Students, up to this point you have worked on giving *written* directions clearly, but it is equally important to be able to communicate clear directions *orally*. So, now you will have an opportunity to do this by giving a Demonstration Talk, a presentation to the class in which you show how to play or build or cook or make something. I have prepared a handout of suggested topics for you [see Figure 3–10], but feel free to choose a different topic that is not on the list.

"These are simply suggestions to get you thinking about what you might want to describe and demonstrate. If you find that you're having trouble coming up with a suitable topic, you might look closely at these *categories* and see if something comes to mind:

- Animals
- Cars
- Computers
- Food
- Games
- Health

Doing a Demonstration Talk

Topics and Techniques for a Successful Presentation

Show how to . . .

- administer first aid
- analyze handwriting
- build a model airplane
- care for skis and/or ski properly
- carve a pumpkin
- create a holiday decoration
- create a Web page
- develop photographs
- give a dog a bath
- make a puppet
- paint a picture
- perform a magic trick
- play a particular sport
- play or care for a musical instrument
- prepare or cook a certain food
- read a musical score
- read a nautical map or chart

Suggestions for a successful presentation:

- Choose a subject that interests you and your audience.
- Explain the subject simply but completely.
- Define key terms.
- Keep the steps in proper order.
- Use examples, charts, details, and/or pictures if appropriate and helpful.

Your Demonstration Talk will be evaluated in three areas:

- Voice—volume; rate; articulation
- Organization—clear directions; informative; sufficient details
- Delivery—natural, poised manner; demonstration proceeds smoothly; competent handling of materials

---

Figure 3–10. Demonstration Talk Topics and Techniques

49

- Hobbies/Leisure Activities
- Holidays
- Jobs/Careers
- Medicine
- Music
- School Subjects
- Sports

"Your demonstration will probably take ten to fifteen minutes, but let me know in advance if you think you will need more time. With advance notice, I can adjust the schedule of student presenters on the day that you will be speaking, and then you won't be rushed for time."

I encourage students to write out in advance the steps and directions involved in their demonstrations. This kind of preparation will help them organize their presentations and consider all the many details involved. If you think your students might need some extra assistance in preparing their Demonstration Talks, you can *require* that students write out their directions in advance and hand them in to you for review. This will give you a chance to intervene with helpful suggestions that might make the demonstration proceed more smoothly.

The students' presentations are evaluated in three areas—Voice, Organization, and Delivery—and the students receive a copy of the evaluation form well in advance of their scheduled talk (see Figure 3–11). This way, students can use this information to help them prepare an organized, informative demonstration.

I have conducted the Demonstration Talk with both junior and senior high classes, and it has proven to be an engaging, entertaining, memorable experience. Students have taken the class to the gym for a demonstration of aerobics or strategies involved in basketball; to the weight room and band room; to the home economics classroom for a cooking demonstration; and outside to the students' parking lot for a demonstration of car-care tips. Other students have engaged their classmates in elaborate paper-folding demonstrations, holiday gift wrapping, card tricks, first-aid demonstrations, and pumpkin carving.

The number of animals that have paraded through my classroom over the years during these talks is pretty impressive, too. Students' pet dogs, cats, and birds have all served, willingly or reluctantly, as the main prop for demonstrations of pet care and animal training. One of these presentations was particularly memorable: A student who belonged to the local 4-H Club was making preparations at the time to participate in an upcoming county fair, so she asked if she could bring in her pet chicken for her talk. She said she would demonstrate to the class the steps she went through to groom and prepare such an animal for exhibition at the fair. I said, "Fine," and looked forward to seeing this cute little pet.

Speaker: _____

Topic: _____

Date: _____ Period: _____

4 – Outstanding
3 – Good
2 – Fair
1 – Needs work

VOICE   1   2   3   4

Volume
Pitch
Rate
Articulation

ORGANIZATION   1   2   3   4

Clear directions
Details
Informative

DELIVERY   1   2   3   4

Natural, poised manner
Good eye contact
Use of hands
Handling of materials

ADDITIONAL COMMENTS

Figure 3–11. Demonstration Talk Evaluation Form

Well, when the time arrived for her scheduled talk, she brought into class this *thing* that looked to be about the size of a four-door sedan. She plopped "Chicken-zilla" on the table in the front of the room, and her classmates suddenly vacated the first four rows of desks. I remember thinking, "Wow! That thing could feed a whole family for weeks—if you counted in the chicken cutlets and chicken soup and chicken sandwiches and . . ." But I didn't think the pet's owner would appreciate my "serving suggestions," so I let it pass.

The Demonstration Talk is an engaging and fun activity that works effectively to improve students' poise and speaking skills in general. In addition, it will do more to help develop students' organization skills than any other speech. Students learn to put their directions into a sequence and to communicate that sequence clearly. Watch out for those chickens, though!

Conclusion

In this chapter I have focused on activities designed to develop students' oral communication competence. You might try conducting these activities one after another in an unbroken sequence as part of a unit; or you could introduce and scatter them throughout the semester at key points in your curriculum. The point is to be sure that you *do* include them in your course. Students' oral communication skills are an integral part of the language arts, and students use these skills constantly to make sense of their learning in all classes. With our help, students will be able to use these skills well.

Notes

1. M. Donaldson, 1978, *Children's Minds* (W. W. Norton & Company), 129.
2. S. Elkind, 1975, *Improvisation Handbook* (Glenview, IL: Scott, Foresman and Company), 11.
3. Elkind, 10–11.
4. Elkind, 18.
5. Elkind, 13.
6. The "One-Way Versus Two-Way Communication" exercise is adapted from J. W. Pfeiffer and J. E. Jones, eds., 1974, *A Handbook of Structured Experiences for Human Relations Training*, Vol. 1, rev. ed. (San Francisco, CA: Jossey-Bass/Pfeiffer), 13–18.

Works Cited

Elkind, S. 1975. *Improvisation Handbook.* Glenview, IL: Scott, Foresman and Company.

Golub, J. N. 1994. *Activities for an Interactive Classroom.* Urbana, IL: National Council of Teachers of English.

Pfeiffer, J. W., and J. E. Jones, eds. 1974. *A Handbook of Structured Experiences for Human Relations Training.* Vol. 1. Rev. ed. San Francisco, CA: Jossey-Bass/Pfeiffer.

Ray, T. J. 1976. "Describing Geometric Forms for Feedback," in *Writing Exercises from* Exercise Exchange, ed. L. Long, 111–14. Urbana, IL: National Council of Teachers of English.

Recommended Resources

Spolin, V. 1963. *Improvisation for the Theater: A Handbook of Teaching and Directing Techniques.* Evanston, IL: Northwestern University Press.

Way, B. 1967. *Development Through Drama.* London: Longmans, Green and Company.

4

Learning in a Small-Group Discussion Setting

It's important to set up instructional situations that engage students in working in small-group settings. Such strategies as group discussions and group projects allow students to construct and negotiate meanings in a social context. They are able to try out their rough-draft ideas on others and revise their interpretations in response to the feedback they receive. Small-group settings, in other words, enable students to use their own talk as a vehicle for meaning making and reflection.

But students don't necessarily come to class with their basic group-discussion skills already mastered. They need help with these skills, and they also need some important information and insights about how to work productively and harmoniously in a small-group setting. The activities described in this chapter can help develop these skills and insights.

A List of Group-Discussion Skills

Learning to work effectively in a small group involves learning about—and practicing—some basic interpersonal communication skills. At some time during a group discussion, a competent member of the group should demonstrate many of the following positive behaviors:

- Speak loudly enough to be heard.
- Ask appropriate questions as well as answer them.
- Contribute and respond, but not dominate the discussion.
- Act as a group leader.
- Help the group reach agreement.

- Stick to the topic.
- Recognize the significance of nonverbal communication.
- Paraphrase and summarize.
- Draw the group back to the topic.
- Check perceptions about the meaning of statements and ideas.
- Initiate discussion.
- Seek people's opinions, especially of those who have not been talking.
- Clarify ideas.
- Motivate other members of the group.
- Brainstorm for ideas.

These, then, are the behaviors and skills that are developed through students' engagement in the following group-discussion activities.

Brainstorming

Having students practice brainstorming ideas in a small-group setting introduces the concept of group discussion and also serves as a community-building strategy. In addition, it is a way to open up students' imaginations and allow students to play with language possibilities. The principle of brainstorming is that this process spurs the mind to come up with new and additional ideas. As words, phrases, and concepts are stated by one person, other people use those contributions as stimuli to come up with their own ideas. Here are the rules for brainstorming and a series of appropriate topics and exercises for brainstorming in small groups as I described them in my 1994 book, *Activities for an Interactive Classroom* (21–24):

Rules for Brainstorming

1. *"The more ideas, the better."*

    In brainstorming, the goal is to generate as many ideas as possible. Have the brainstorming groups of students create a long list of suggestions and possibilities; the longer the list, the better. The *quality* of the ideas can be evaluated later. At a later time—and in a separate operation—the "bad" ideas can be separated from the "good" ones. But in the beginning, students should consider anything and everything related to the topic being brainstormed. To encourage the production of as many ideas as possible, you might set up a competitive arrangement between the brainstorming groups in the classroom. After each brainstorming session, ask the recorder in each group to add up all the ideas on his or her list. Write the totals for each group—as reported by the group's recorder—on the board.

2. *"The wilder the ideas, the better."*

This is an opportunity for students to think of crazy, silly, outrageous ideas. Such thinking is encouraged in this activity and in this environment. Because students are building on each other's ideas here, one student's "crazy" suggestion may give a classmate a terrific idea that would not have been thought of without the "crazy" stimulus.

3. *"'Hitchhiking' is encouraged."*

Brainstorming involves an intense cooperative effort in that students work with each other's ideas and suggestions. Students are encouraged to "hitchhike" on each other's ideas, modifying classmates' suggestions in different ways in order to generate other ideas. With this arrangement, students must be cautioned not to see an idea as "theirs." That great idea they thought of probably arose because of something they heard from a classmate. So whose idea is it, really? All generated ideas should be seen as belonging to the *group,* and all are available for modification and improvement without a need to claim "ownership."

As an example of how hitchhiking can work to produce something valuable, I once had a class brainstorm ways to improve a standard piece of classroom furniture, the common student desk. At one point in the brainstorming, I overheard a student in a group say, "Throw it off the face of the earth." Immediately another student exclaimed, "Hey! Let's put a map of the earth *in* the desk, right on the top desk part." And another student added to this idea, "Yeah, and we can have rollers that you can use to turn the map to any part of the earth you want to see." This is a nice idea, and it came about because of the original suggestion to throw the desk off the face of the earth. You can use this example with students to show them how *wild* ideas and *hitchhiking* can work together to produce something that later proves to be pertinent, practical, and valuable.

4. *"No evaluation of ideas during brainstorming."*

This is the rule that makes everything else possible. If students were to evaluate ideas as they were being generated, the process would come to a halt quickly. Imagine a student offering a suggestion only to be told, "*That's not on the topic,*" or "*That's stupid!*" That would be the last time the student would offer *anything.* Who wants to risk being told that their idea is "wrong" or "silly"? Simply instruct the group recorders to write down *everything;* they can evaluate and eliminate *later.*

Procedure for Brainstorming

Each brainstorming session should last three minutes—enough time for students to generate lots of ideas, but short enough that students don't get tired or bored with

the activity. Each subsequent brainstorming session should have the groups produc-
ing a greater number of ideas than they did in the previous one. As the groups are
brainstorming, call out the time remaining in thirty-second intervals. This keeps
the brainstorming at an intense level of activity. At the end of three minutes, direct
all groups to stop immediately; have the recorders count the number of brain-
stormed ideas on their lists; and write the totals for each group on the board for
everyone to see.

Sample Topics for Brainstorming

The following topics may be used to allow students to practice the brainstorming
process:

1. How many ways can you think of to come to school in the morning? (Pogo-
    stick, donkey, parachute, rocket ship, walk over the telephone wires, etc.)
2. Assuming you could change your size and shape, how would you come to
    school in the morning? (Change into a drop of water and come to school in
    the drinking fountain; come to school in your friend's lunch sack, etc.)
3. How many ways can you think of to have fun with an alligator? (Put dry ice
    in his mouth and call the fire department; buy him a big red balloon at the
    fair; play jump rope with him; etc.)
4. How many different kinds of *lines* can you think of? (Lines you have to
    memorize for a drama production; lines on a football field; lines that form
    as people wait to get into a movie; etc.)
5. List everything you can think of that is both *soft* and *blue*. (Melted blue
    crayons; a fish that is dipped in blue paint; a sad teddy bear; etc.)
6. Make a list of things that come in, or are associated with, the number
    three. (Three blind mice; three little pigs; three sides of a triangle; triple-
    decker sandwich; etc.)

During the first few brainstorming sessions, emphasize only the *number* of
ideas generated, trying to get the students to increase the amount of ideas suggested and the length of their lists in each subsequent round of brainstorming.
Within three or four sessions—each lasting three minutes and using different topics each time—you should find that students can generate more than one hundred
ideas. At this point, you can begin to *look* at some of these ideas by giving additional instructions. Use the following topic for this purpose:

> "Your group is an advertising agency. A certain manufacturer of a popular kind of
> candy has come to you because it has plans to redesign its product. The manufac-
> turer will change the packaging, for instance, but it also wants to change the *name* of
> the candy. That's why it has come to you for help. In three minutes, brainstorm pos-
> sible names for M & M's candies."

At the end of this brainstorming session, have the group's recorders add up the total number of items on their list, and then give these additional instructions to each group:

> "Go through your list and select three of your *best* names for M & M's candies. These should be ideas that you think are so unique and unusual that they just might work as suitable alternatives to the candy's current name. Take a few minutes to decide which three names on your list you like the best, and then we'll hear these selections from each group."

Once students have become familiar with the brainstorming process and have experienced a few trial runs using the rules and topics listed above, they are ready to do more extensive work in small groups. They will still use the skills they have just practiced, but now their minds are more open to the ideas of playing with possibilities and considering a variety of alternatives. Try the following exercise and project as a follow-up to the initial brainstorming sessions. . . . [It] will allow students to further develop the brainstorming skills they have been practicing. . . .

A Brainstorming Project

> "Design a new eating implement that has as important a function as the knife, fork, and spoon. This invention belongs on every dining room table."

Have students complete the following tasks:

1. Design the invention and be prepared to explain to the class how it works. Feel free to draw a picture if you wish.
2. Give your invention a name.
3. In an oral presentation, convince the rest of the class that your invention is (a) necessary, (b) practical, and (c) desirable.
4. Design a magazine ad for your invention. (You might have students write a radio ad, too, and then comment on the differences in the demands and problems encountered in dealing with the two media. Consider also the idea of having students create a TV ad for their product and then act out the ad in front of the class.)

Each group in turn presents its design for a new eating implement to the class, describing how the invention works and persuading the class that the implement is necessary, practical, and desirable. By the time this project is completed, the students will have demonstrated mastery of the brainstorming skills and process. . . .

The "Cooperation Squares" Game[1]

Cooperation is a key element in any group-discussion activity. Thus, students need to be made aware of the importance of this trait and have an opportunity to practice or rehearse cooperative behavior. The "Cooperation Squares" game serves both to raise students' awareness and provide an experience in which cooperative behavior is required in order to complete the task successfully.

Some preparation of materials is needed in advance of conducting this activity. Prepare several sets of squares as shown in Figure 4–1. Each set consists of five envelopes containing pieces of stiff paper cut into patterns that will form five six-by-six-inch squares. You will need one set of the five different squares for each group of five students. Cut each square into the parts *a* through *j* and lightly pencil in the letters. Then mark the envelopes A through E and distribute the pieces in this way:

Envelope A: pieces i, h, e
Envelope B: pieces a, a, a, c

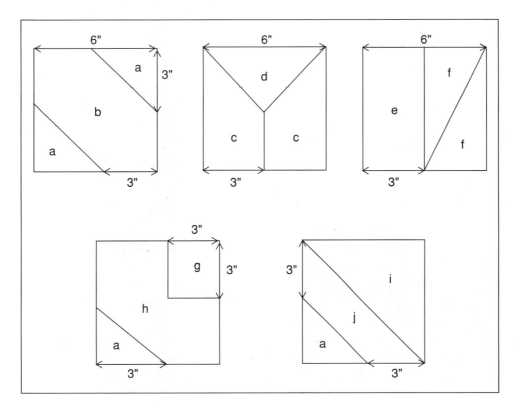

Figure 4–1. The "Cooperation Squares" Game (Patterns)

Envelope C: pieces a, j
Envelope D: pieces d, f
Envelope E: pieces g, b, f, c

Just before putting the pieces into the envelopes as indicated above, erase the small letters from the pieces and write instead the envelope letters A through E so that the pieces can be easily returned to the proper envelopes after the exercise.

Now you're ready to run the exercise.

Direct students to assemble in groups of five persons each. Any students left over, which could be between one and four students, can serve as observers, and their observations of the groups' behaviors will be reported at the conclusion of the exercise. Distribute one set of five envelopes to each group so that each person has one envelope, instructing students not to open the envelopes until told to do so. And now the directions to the students:

> "Students, this is an exercise in *cooperation.* Each of you has in front of you an envelope containing pieces of a puzzle. The pieces in all five envelopes, when put together correctly, will form five squares of equal size. And that is the task of your group—to form those five squares. Your task is not completed until everyone in the group has in front of him or her a perfect square, and all the squares are of the same size.
>
> "There are two rules that you must observe while putting the pieces of the puzzle together:
>
> • No talking is allowed.
> • No member of the group may ask for a piece from another member; nor can you signal in any way that you want one. You must wait until that member sees that you need the piece and gives it to you. In other words, you can only *give* pieces; you cannot *take* them.
>
> "At this time, you may open your envelopes and begin."

This is a fascinating activity to observe in progress because of its particular design. For instance, it is possible for group members to assemble several different *individual* combinations of squares, but only one total combination will allow the formation of all five squares simultaneously. Thus, it often happens that one group member will assemble a square quickly and then sit back and simply wait for the other members to catch up and complete *their* squares. But, unless this member's particular square is put together with the right combination of pieces, it will need to be disassembled at some point so that the other members can complete their own squares and the group task.

Watch closely the behavior of this group member who has finished assembling a square early. At some point, he or she will notice the other group members struggling with the remaining pieces and suddenly realize, "Hey, wait a minute! One of the pieces of *my* square is needed to make a square over there." Reluctantly, the member will disassemble his or her square and hand over one of the crucial pieces. And that is when the rest of the group will finally begin to make substantial progress. It's an interesting phenomenon to observe.

When all or most of the groups have finished, stop the activity and engage the students in discussion and reflection. Ask the students such questions as

- How did your group get the task completed?
- How well did your group members work together?
- What was the most difficult part of this exercise for you?
- How did you feel when someone held a piece and did not see that it was needed somewhere else?
- What was your reaction when someone finished his or her square and then sat back without seeing whether his or her solution prevented others from assembling their squares?
- What were your feelings if you finished your square and then began to realize that you would have to break it up and give away a piece?
- Was there a certain group climate that helped or hindered?

At this point, you may wish to invite the student observers to report their findings and reactions. The last and most important issue for discussion is the insight to be learned from this activity: that a group completes its task by engaging in *cooperative* behavior. This means that its members are being observant of—and attending to—the needs of one another as they work to accomplish their task.

The "Moon Survival" Exercise[2]

An important skill in almost any group discussion is the ability to reach agreement. When you are working alone, it's fairly easy to reach agreement: you just look in the mirror and say, "Oh, you are sooo right!" And you are. But, when you get together in a group of two to four other people, you find that everyone else thinks he or she is right, too, and so disagreements occur. This activity can help students learn to resolve their disagreements and reach consensus.

The "Moon Survival" exercise is an old one, but I include it here because it is an extremely effective way to engage students in practicing and developing the skills involved in reaching agreement. In addition, I have designed a variation for this activity—an extra step that makes the exercise even more involving and effective for the students. First, the original version.

Step 1

In this activity, students must rank order certain items. Hand out copies of the "Decision Form" sheet that describes the situation and gives the instructions (see Figure 4–2).

In the first step, students should rank order the items *individually*—no checking with their classmates or asking any questions. They simply work alone, recording their best estimate of each item's value in helping the crew make the two-hundred-mile trip on the moon's surface.

Step 2

After all students have completed their individual ranking of the items, they should assemble in groups of four to five people each. The size of the groups is important: A group composed of only three students does not allow for enough differences of opinion, and a group of six or more is simply too large. Students will either withdraw from the discussion or break into subgroups and start their own conversation. Hand out one more copy of the "Decision Form" sheet to each group (one sheet per group). Then explain to them:

> "Now you are going to rank order these items as a group. You may find this task difficult because there are sure to be some disagreements about the relative importance of these items. But this is the point of the exercise—learning how to resolve such disagreements and reach consensus. Here are some guidelines to follow as you engage in your discussion."

Hand out copies of the sheet "Reaching Group Decisions by Consensus" (see Figure 4–3), and review the guidelines with the class before turning them loose to begin their discussion.

After going over the guidelines, direct the groups to begin their deliberations and record their rank-ordering decisions on the group form passed out earlier. In a reflective discussion after all groups have completed their group rankings, you might ask such questions as

- What was the most difficult part of this exercise for you?
- What strategies did you use to reach agreement on the various items?
- Did the leadership rotate among group members? Or did one person seem to act as leader most of the time?
- Did all group members stay active and involved? Or did a few members do most of the work?
- What did you learn from this activity about ways to reach agreement in a group?

The "Moon Survival" Exercise

Decision Form

INSTRUCTIONS: You are in a space crew originally scheduled to rendezvous with a mother ship on the lighted surface of the moon. Due to mechanical difficulties, however, your ship was forced to land at a spot some 200 miles from the rendezvous point. During reentry and landing, much of the equipment aboard was damaged, and, since survival depends upon reaching the mother ship, the most critical items available must be chosen for the 200-mile trip. Below are listed the 15 items left intact and undamaged after landing. Your task is to rank order them in terms of their importance in allowing your crew to reach the rendezvous point. Place the number 1 beside the most important item, the number 2 beside the second most important, and so on through 15, the least important.

_____ Box of Matches

_____ Food Concentrate

_____ 50 Feet of Nylon Rope

_____ Parachute Silk

_____ Portable Heating Unit

_____ Two .45-Caliber Pistols

_____ One Case Dehydrated Pet Milk

_____ Two 100-lb. Tanks of Oxygen

_____ Stellar Map of the Moon's Constellation

_____ Life Raft

_____ Magnetic Compass

_____ 5 Gallons of Water

_____ Signal Flares

_____ First-Aid Kit Containing Injection Needles

_____ Solar-Powered FM Receiver-Transmitter

Figure 4–2. The "Moon Survival" Exercise: Decision Form

The "Moon Survival" Exercise

Reaching Group
Decisions by Consensus

This is an exercise in group decision making. Your group is to employ the method of Group Consensus in reaching its decision. This means that the selection and rank placement for each of the items MUST be agreed upon by each group member before it becomes a part of the group decision.

Consensus is difficult to reach. Therefore, not every ranking will meet with everyone's *complete* approval. Try, as a group, to make each ranking one with which ALL group members can at least partially agree.

Here are some guidelines to use in reaching agreements:

- Avoid arguing for your own individual judgments. Approach the task on the basis of logic.

- Avoid changing your mind ONLY in order to reach agreement and avoid conflict. Support only solutions with which you are able to agree somewhat at least.

- Avoid conflict-reducing techniques such as majority vote, averaging, or trading in reaching decisions.

- View differences of opinion as helpful rather than as a hindrance in decision making.

Figure 4–3. The "Moon Survival" Exercise: Guidelines for Reaching Consensus

Step 3

Now hand out the Answer Key (see Figure 4–4) that shows the rank ordering of the items by NASA administrators, complete with a rationale for each ranking. This is the first time that students learn that an Answer Key even exists. I don't think they would have worked with such commitment during the first two stages of this activity if they had known that they were trying to figure out predetermined answers. But now that they have completed their individual and group rankings, they enjoy comparing their decisions with the responses of the experts.

Step 4

This is the final step in the original version of this exercise and the source of a major insight for the participants. Hand out the "Data Sheet" (see Figure 4–5) and have all students fill in the columns. In the column "Your Rank," students write the rank order of the items that they completed when working alone. In the "Group Rank" column, each student in the group fills in the same numbers—the rankings they listed for the items as a group.

Then the students should find the "differences"—first between "Your Rank" and the "KEY," and then between the "Group Rank" and the "KEY." The two columns of differences should be added and the totals listed at the bottom of the sheet. Students should find that the group decisions are more accurate (closer to the KEY answer) than are any of their individual decisions.

An important insight that students should gain from this activity is that group discussion is valuable because it enables members to learn from one another and gain information and insights that will help produce a better product or result in the end. In most cases, the "Group Rank" is closer to the "KEY" than any single member's individual ranking because the group work allows members the opportunity to get answers to their questions and to revise their initial thoughts and rankings. The operation of multiple perspectives in a group tends to result in more realistic and thoughtful decisions, and this activity highlights this principle.

A Variation

One element that is missing from the structure of the "Moon Survival" exercise above is a "fishbowl" arrangement, whereby students seated in an *outside* circle observe the discussion of participants seated in an *inner* circle. This arrangement is valuable because it allows the student observers to reflect on various discussion behaviors and evaluate their effectiveness. It is difficult for students to engage in any reflection while they are working as a member of a group (as in Step 2 above); they are too involved in presenting their own opinions and responding to the

The "Moon Survival" Exercise
KEY

___15___ Box of Matches (little or no use on moon)

___4___ Food Concentrate (supply daily food required)

___6___ 50 Feet of Nylon Rope (useful in tying injured together, help in climbing)

___8___ Parachute Silk (shelter against sun's rays)

___13___ Portable Heating Unit (useful only if party landed on dark side)

___11___ Two .45-Caliber Pistols (self-propulsion devices could be made from them)

___12___ One Case Dehydrated Pet Milk (food, mixed with water for drinking)

___1___ Two 100-lb. Tanks of Oxygen (fills respiration requirement)

___3___ Stellar Map of the Moon's Constellation (one of the principal ways of finding directions)

___9___ Life Raft (carbon dioxide bottles for self-propulsion across chasms, etc.)

___14___ Magnetic Compass (probably no magnetized poles, thus useless)

___2___ 5 Gallons of Water (replenishes loss by perspiring, etc.)

___10___ Signal Flares (distress call when line of sight possible)

___7___ First-Aid Kit Containing Injection Needles (oral pills or injection medicine valuable)

___5___ Solar-Powered FM Receiver-Transmitter (distress signal transmitter, possible communication with mother ship)

Figure 4–4. The "Moon Survival" Exercise: Answer Key

ITEMS	Your Rank	Difference	KEY	Difference	Group Rank
The Moon Survival Excercise					
Data Sheet					
Box of Matches			15		
Food Concentrate			4		
50 Feet of Nylon Rope			6		
Parachute Silk			8		
Portable Heating Unit			13		
Two .45-Caliber Pistols			11		
Dehydrated Pet Milk			12		
Tanks of Oxygen			1		
Stellar Map			3		
Life Raft			9		
Magnetic Compass			14		
5 Gallons of Water			2		
Signal Flares			10		
First-Aid Kit			7		
Receiver-Transmitter			5		
TOTALS of "Difference" columns					

You should find that the group decisions are more accurate (closer to the KEY answer) than are any of your individual decisions.

Figure 4–5. The "Moon Survival" Exercise: Data Sheet

views of others. So, I designed a variation of the "Moon Survival" exercise—an extra step—to build in a fishbowl arrangement and thus provide an opportunity for observation, reflection, and evaluation.

The variation begins after the completion of Step 2 above and before Step 3. At this point, students have just completed their group ranking of the items, and they are still unaware of the Answer Key and its rankings. In this variation, the activity in Step 4 above is dropped, and the Answer Key is not presented until after the completion of the following alternate activity.

Step 3a (replaces Steps 3 and 4 above) While the students are still working in their groups to create a group ranking of the items, begin assembling a circle of empty chairs either in the center of the classroom or at the front. The circle should be easily visible by all groups, and the number of chairs should equal the number of groups that are working. When most of the groups have completed their ranking, get the students' attention and give the directions for the next activity:

"Students, at this time, would each group please appoint a representative or negotiator from your group to come and sit in this circle of chairs?

[After representatives are seated in the circle] "Your representatives are now going to try to reach agreement on a rank order for these items. While they are engaged in discussion, you are free to talk among yourselves in your own groups, but you cannot communicate with your representative.

"Certainly there will be moments during the discussion when you *do* want to talk to your representative. Perhaps you want to give him or her some information or a persuasive argument that he or she can then present to the inner circle; maybe you want to suggest that he or she change his or her stand on how a certain item should be ranked; or you might even want to change representatives and put in another member of your group.

"No problem. Simply yell 'BREAK!' and I will immediately stop the discussion among the negotiators. *All* representatives—not just the one whose group called a break—will go back to their groups and will have thirty seconds for a conference. After thirty seconds, the representatives—either the same or a different person from each group—must return to the inner circle and resume discussion.

"The rule about breaks is that each group can have only two breaks per decision. This means, for instance, that when the negotiators begin their discussion, each group may call a break twice while the negotiators are deciding which item should be ranked number one. Once that decision is made, each group gets two more breaks allotted to it, which it may use at any time during the deliberations about the number two item.

"The breaks do not carry over from one decision (or 'round') to the next. Even if you do not use both breaks during one round of deliberations, you still have a total of only two breaks during the next round. The breaks do not accumulate from one round to the next.

"Guard your breaks carefully. If you should use up your two breaks early in a particular round's discussion, you could be stuck with no way to communicate important information to your representative until that round's decision is made. Once you have used up your two breaks, you will be dependent on other groups to call a break in order to talk to your representative."

Note: When I first started running this variation, I allowed the groups to have as many breaks as they wanted. They could yell "BREAK!" *anytime* they felt that they had something to communicate to their representative. After hearing the groups call "BREAK!" about every seven seconds, however, I began to suspect that maybe this wasn't such a good idea, so I changed to the "two-breaks-per-decision" rule and found that the negotiators' discussion proceeded much more smoothly.

There are instructions specifically for the negotiators, too:

"Even though you are serving as a representative from your group, you should feel free to change your mind in response to comments and insights from the other representatives during the discussion. You do *not* have to stick with the rank ordering made by your 'outside' group if you think a different item is a better choice at some point. If your group doesn't like the decisions you're making, it can always 'recall' you by calling for a break and changing representatives. But, as long as you're serving as a negotiator here, you should be your own person and make your own decisions."

And so it begins. The group's representatives in the inner circle engage in discussion, trying to reach agreement on the rank ordering of items, while the students in the outside groups listen intently, knowing they can participate and influence the course of the discussion through the breaks available to them.

But, because you have set up a fishbowl arrangement, you, the teacher, have an opportunity to intervene at appropriate moments to improve students' group-discussion behavior. Both the students in the inside circle and the outside groups will benefit from your coaching. You might intervene when

- One student interrupts another: "Ellen, wait a minute! You interrupted Xinia. She hadn't finished explaining her position yet. That's not fair! Okay, let's go back, and Xinia, finish what you were saying."
- It's time to find out if the negotiators are close to agreement: "It sounds as if a number of you have changed your opinion about which item should be ranked as number four. Let's go around the circle, and each of you in turn, just tell us which item you want for number four. Don't give us a reason for your choice right now. Just identify which item you have in mind."

- Negotiators are deadlocked: arguments have gone on for quite some time, but no compromise or other movement toward agreement is occurring. "Students, we're hearing the same arguments over and over, and no one is changing his or her mind. Would you begin talking about *how* you're going to reach agreement about which item to list next? In other words, I'm asking you to drop from the *task* level— 'Which item should be ranked number seven?'—to the *group maintenance* level—'What are some strategies we can use to reach agreement on this issue?' Make that your topic of discussion now."

And you will probably find many more reasons to intervene, too. The point is that you want the negotiators to adhere to exemplary group-discussion behavior even when confronted with strong convictions and opposing views. After several interventions on your part in the early rounds of discussion, you will find that the students' interruptions of classmates will become fewer and the progress toward agreement on the items will become increasingly steady and smooth.

Even during the thirty-second breaks, there are things you can do to move this activity along. Perhaps one group has had the same representative in the inner circle for the past fifteen minutes. You might go to that group and suggest that it change negotiators simply to get more of its group members involved. Or you can quietly suggest an argument or a strategy to a negotiator as a way to introduce a new idea that might produce some movement toward consensus.

The strategies that my students used to reach agreement were wide-ranging: Sometimes the negotiators would agree that they weren't getting anywhere trying to select the next item, so they would decide to rank order the *least* important item instead and work backward from there. Other sessions had the negotiators rank ordering two items at once to resolve a disagreement. Often students would show up in class with a dictionary or encyclopedia or magazine article to prove the point that they had been trying to make the day before.

As you can imagine, this variation of the "Moon Survival" activity takes up a considerable amount of class time. For example, I have run this activity several times, with both junior and senior high school students, and the average time to complete the "negotiator" phase of this exercise has been about a week—five consecutive class sessions of fifty minutes each.

The longest negotiation session I've ever had lasted two weeks. Students got to the point where they'd come into class and set up the chairs for the inner circle even before the bell had rung to start class. The negotiators would immediately resume their discussion from the previous day, and the first break would be called before I had even finished taking attendance. Each day they brought in new arguments and evidence, and each day I heard complaints from my colleagues at school about my students talking about "this moon stuff" while in their other classes. So, I don't know exactly how long the activity will take to complete when you run it yourself. But, I think you will find that this instructional horse will give you and your students a fine, engaging, and worthwhile ride.

The Alligator River Problem[3]

The Alligator River Problem is another rank-ordering activity that can reinforce the decision-making skills developed by the "Moon Survival" exercise. It can also be used instead of the "Moon Survival" activity if you are pressed for time and need a shorter instructional strategy that still deals with the same skills. I have designed this activity so that it can also serve as an introduction to the structure and techniques of a persuasion paper (see Steps 5 and 6 below).

The Alligator River Problem is a cleverly constructed story that poses an intriguing, complex dilemma. Students meet five characters who display undesirable social traits and must rank order these characters in terms of their behavior. The character ranked number one should be the most rotten, most disgusting, worst person of all. The students become engaged in a discussion of values: Which is worse—violence, indifference, betrayal, ingratitude, or . . . ? Well, this story has just about everything!

> DIRECTIONS: After reading the story below, list the five characters according to the following standard:
>
> 1. should be the most rotten, most disgusting, worst person of all
> 2. should be a little bit better
> 3. should be somewhat better
> 4. comes close to being the best of the bunch
> 5. should be the best person you can pick from all five

Once upon a time there lived a girl named Abigail who was in love with a boy named Gregory. Gregory had an unfortunate accident and broke his glasses. Abigail, being a true friend, volunteered to take them to be repaired. But the repair shop was across the dangerous Alligator River, and during a sudden flood, the bridge was washed away.

Poor Gregory could see nothing without his glasses, so Abigail was desperate to get across the river to the repair shop. While she was standing sadly on the bank of the river, clutching the broken glasses in her hands, a boy named Sinbad glided by in a rowboat.

She asked Sinbad if he would take her across. He agreed to do it on condition that while she was having the glasses repaired, she would go to a nearby store and steal a transistor radio that he had been wanting. Abigail refused to do such a thing and went to see a friend named Ivan who had a boat.

When Abigail told Ivan her problem, he refused to help her in any way. He said he was too busy and besides, he didn't want to get involved in any way with anything to do with Sinbad. Abigail, worried about Gregory and feeling that she now had no other choice, returned to Sinbad and told him she would have to agree to his plan.

Well, Sinbad took Abigail across the terrible river; she stole the radio for him and got the glasses fixed and returned finally to Gregory. She gave him the glasses and told him what she had had to do in order to get across the river. Shocked and horrified, Gregory told her that he would have nothing to do with a thief and said he never wanted to see her again!

Abigail, upset and crying, turned to her last friend, Slug, with her sad story. Slug was very sorry for Abigail, and he promised her he would get even with Gregory. They went to Gregory's house where Slug beat Gregory up and broke his glasses again as Abigail watched and laughed joyously.

Step 1

Immediately after hearing the story, students should rank order the five characters in terms of their behavior. Once again, number one is "the most rotten, most disgusting, worst person of all." Just as they did in the first part of the "Moon Survival" exercise, students should complete this step *alone* without checking or sharing responses with their classmates.

Step 2

Students should assemble in groups of four to five people each and begin trying to achieve a group ranking of the five characters. This means that each member must agree with the decision before it is recorded. Both Steps 1 and 2 here are similar to the first two steps in the "Moon Survival" exercise. If you are conducting this activity without having first run the "Moon Survival," be sure to introduce the guidelines "Reaching Group Decisions by Consensus" (see Figure 4–3) at this time.

Step 3

Ask each group to share its group ranking with the class and give an explanation for its number one selection. It is quite possible that not all groups will have completed their rankings, since this is an exercise in value-laden personal choices and attitudes. But that's okay; the most important thing is that the groups will have been engaged in a sharing of views and an attempt to reach agreement, both processes involving the practice of several small-group discussion behaviors and skills.

Step 4

Each student, working alone, writes a position paper, identifying which character he or she thinks is the worst and explaining his or her choice. Students should try to be as persuasive as possible. One or two paragraphs should be sufficient.

Step 5

When they are finished writing, students should put their position papers on top of three or four blank sheets of paper and staple all sheets together.

Directions to students:

"In just a moment, you will trade papers with a classmate. When you get your classmate's paper, read it carefully and then write a response on the first blank sheet that's stapled to the paper. You can agree with your classmate's position, offering additional information in support; or you can disagree with your classmate's choice of character, presenting your own perspective; perhaps offer some arguments that your classmate failed to consider; or in some other way, comment on what he or she has written.

"When you are finished writing a response to that paper, stand up and trade papers with someone else who has also finished writing and is standing up. When you get this second paper, you can respond not only to the original position paper on top, but also to the first respondent's comment. Simply add your own thoughts, agreeing or disagreeing, and present your own arguments and perspective.

"And that's what we will do for the next twenty minutes—trade the papers around, responding to the original position statements and to the comments and questions that appear on the response sheets, and contribute to the growing conversations on each paper."

You should find that the students engage in the above writing and responding enthusiastically because it is *authentic* communication: Students have something to say and someone to say it *to*. There is a real audience and a real purpose for their communication.

Step 6

After about twenty minutes, direct students to return the papers to their "owners," the writers of the original position papers.

Directions to students:

"First, read over the responses and conversation that has been generated by your position paper. Then revise your original explanation and rationale for your choice, taking into account some of the arguments raised by your respondents. In your revision, you can change your selection of the worst character, or you can strengthen your original position by responding to some of the more insightful points made by your classmates on the response sheets. But, use the conversation on your response sheets to make your position more persuasive and convincing."

The final position papers should be substantially new and improved over the initial drafts, and the authentic conversations in writing will have helped make them so.

The Maze: A Game of Decisions and Actions and Values

About twenty years ago, I saw the following description of The Maze game in a local, independent newspaper in Seattle. Although I have since lost the source for this activity, I have continued to use this exercise as an integral part of my group-discussion unit because of its effectiveness in developing students' interpersonal and small-group discussion skills.

The Maze, subtitled A Game of Decisions and Actions and Values, engages students in an activity that can be either competitive or cooperative, depending on the students' perceptions and behavior. In fact, this is one of the important points to explore during the postgame discussion. How the students approach and play this game is very revealing of the students' attitudes and values, and these traits will be made visible to the students themselves through this exercise.

What Is It?

The Maze is similar to the game tic-tac-toe. The goal is to create an uninterrupted path across the maze (see Figure 4–6). As in tic-tac-toe, you are allowed one move at a time, and your move can fill any open space. Unlike tic-tac-toe, you are faced with three other players and some rule changes that allow players to trade spaces and take consecutive turns.

How to Play

Divide into four teams. The goal of the North Team is to get to the southern border. The goal of East Team is to get west. The West wants to go east, and the South wants to go north.

Appoint someone to be "maze controller." The controller is responsible for keeping time for each round, collecting moves from each team, and marking the moves on the maze.

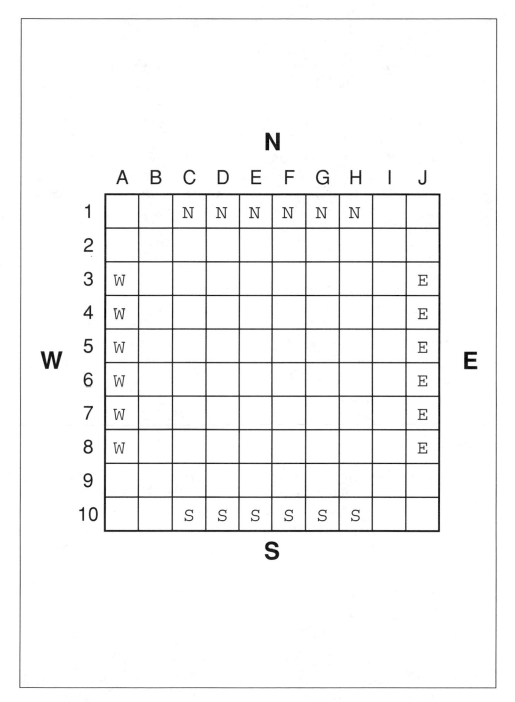

Figure 4–6. The Maze

Rounds One–Four

During rounds one through four, the teams act on their own. Each round lasts five minutes. At the end of the five-minute decision time, the teams *simultaneously* present their moves to the controller. The moves must be given to the controller on a sheet indicating the coordinates of the space the group wants (see Figure 4–7). *The move must be agreed to by every team member.* If a team can't make a consensus decision, it loses its turn.

The controller then places the moves on the maze by placing the letter of each team in the space it has requested. If two or more teams choose to move onto the same space, the controller declares this a "deadlock" and voids that move for those two teams. Each team contending for the same space therefore loses its turn.

Rounds Five–Seven

Starting at round five, each team selects a negotiator. At the direction of his or her team, the negotiator can meet with other negotiators to plan trades and strategy moves. The controller calls a halt to each negotiation session after ten minutes and the following team decision session after five minutes.

The controller then collects and posts team moves as in previous rounds. In round five and any subsequent rounds, teams can trade spaces by marking their move card "Team _____ trades space _____ for Team _____'s space _____." If both teams give the controller sheets that match, the trade is allowable.

Round Eight

In round eight—and all future rounds—each team gives to the controller *two consecutive moves* marked with the appropriate round number. Following the negotiation and decision session, the controller collects both moves but marks the board according to how the players moved in sequential rounds. The game concludes when a team succeeds in crossing the maze or a deadlock occurs in which no team can move or trade.

Some Things to Discuss

- Who won?
- How did they do it?
- What role did competition play in the game?
- What did it feel like being the team negotiator and team member?
- Is there a way in which everyone could have won?
- What values does the game explore?

TEAM _____

Round 1 _____

Round 2 _____

Round 3 _____

Round 4 _____

Round 5 _____ (or)

      Team _____ trades space _____ for Team _____'s space _____ .

Round 6 _____ (or)

      Team _____ trades space _____ for Team _____'s space _____ .

Round 7 _____ (or)

      Team _____ trades space _____ for Team _____'s space _____ .

Round 8 . . . Listen for new directions.

Figure 4–7. The Maze: Team Sheet for Recording Moves

Conclusion

When students work together in small-group settings, they are able to use their own talk as a means of learning and negotiating meanings. They have opportunities to try out their emerging interpretations and insights on their classmates and to give and receive help with the coursework. But such group work requires the exercise of certain basic oral communication skills, and these skills must be rehearsed and developed before students can use them to perform their group work successfully. The several activities in this chapter allow for such rehearsal and practice. They are low-risk, engaging exercises that make the invisible communication skills visible to the students, allowing students to gain a measure of control over these desired behaviors.

Notes

1. The "Cooperation Squares" game appeared originally in A. Bavelas, 1950, "Communication Patterns in Task-Oriented Groups," *Journal of the Acoustical Society of America* 22 (6): 725–30. Since then, it has appeared in various forms in several articles and speech communication textbooks, including the following sources: D. Weitzman, 1974, "Break the Ice with Five Squares," *Learning* 3 (1): 32–37; G. Stanford and A. E. Roark, 1974, *Human Interaction in Education* (Boston, MA: Allyn and Bacon), 112–14; J. W. Pfeiffer and J. E. Jones, eds., 1974, *A Handbook of Structured Experiences for Human Relations Training,* vol. 1, rev. ed. (San Francisco, CA: Jossey-Bass/Pfeiffer), 25–30.
2. J. Hall and W. H. Watson, 1970, "The Effects of a Normative Intervention on Group Decision-Making Performance," *Human Relations* 23 (4): 299–317. See also J. Hall, 1971, "Decisions, Decisions, Decisions," *Psychology Today* 5 (6): 51–54, 86–88.
3. S. B. Simon, L. W. Howe, and H. Kirschenbaum, 1972, *Values Clarification: A Handbook of Practical Strategies for Teachers and Students* (New York: Hart), 290–94.

References Consulted

Bavelas, A. 1950. "Communication Patterns in Task-Oriented Groups." *Journal of the Acoustical Society of America* 22 (6): 725–30.

Golub, J. N. 1994. *Activities for an Interactive Classroom.* Urbana, IL: National Council of Teachers of English.

Hall, J. 1971. "Decisions, Decisions, Decisions." *Psychology Today* 5 (6): 51–54, 86–88.

Hall, J., and W. H. Watson. 1970. "The Effects of a Normative Intervention on Group Decision-Making Performance." *Human Relations* 23 (4): 299–317.

Pfeiffer, J. W., and J. E. Jones, eds. 1974. *A Handbook of Structured Experiences for Human Relations Training*. Vol. 1. Rev. ed. San Francisco, CA: Jossey-Bass/Pfeiffer, 25–30.

Simon, S. B., L. W. Howe, and H. Kirschenbaum. 1972. *Values Clarification: A Handbook of Practical Strategies for Teachers and Students*. New York: Hart.

Stanford, G., and A. E. Roark. 1974. *Human Interaction in Education*. Boston, MA: Allyn and Bacon, 112–14.

Weitzman, D. 1974. "Break the Ice with Five Squares." *Learning* 3 (1): 32–37.

5

Speaking of Participles and Gerbils

DIRECTIONS: Punctuate the following letter in two different ways to create opposite meanings.

Dear John,

I want a man who knows what love is all about you are generous kind thoughtful people who are not like you admit to being useless and inferior John you have ruined me for other men I yearn for you I have no feelings whatsoever when we're apart I can be forever happy will you let me be yours

—*Gloria*[1]

The issues involved in the teaching of grammar are of real concern to both beginning and experienced teachers: How much grammar should be taught to students? When should it be taught? How can it be taught in ways that are effective and engaging?

I faced these issues when I created a traditional English grammar course specifically for our English education students. A state of Florida requirement calls for all future English teachers to take such a course as part of their preparation. So, shortly after coming to the university in 1991, I designed a grammar course specifically for our English education students in which they could learn not only the basics of grammar, but also some alternatives to traditional grammar instruction that they could use when they began their own teaching.

First Class Session

It happens every semester when the students come to the first class session of this grammar course: they have this look in their eyes that says, in effect, "Abandon all hope, ye who enter here." I ask them to imagine what the final exam for this course must be like, and they all nod sadly in agreement, recalling their previous school experiences with grammar tests and instruction. Then I say to them:

> "Well, then, why don't we get the final exam out of the way right now, and then you won't have to worry about it throughout the semester."

And so that's what we do: we take the final exam on the first day of class. It's a test that consists of seventeen multiple-choice items, all dealing with a single sentence:

> I have a little shadow that goes in and out with me and what can be the use of him is more than I can see.

I found this test in an NCTE volume, *Measuring Growth in English,* written in 1974 by Paul Diederich. Not that the test is difficult, but the first time I tried taking it, I got only six or seven items correct. I've gotten much better since then, of course, and now I can answer at least eight items correctly.

Try taking it yourself and see how you do:

Traditional English Grammar
Final Exam

DIRECTIONS: Circle the number of the best answer to each question. The test is based on *one* sentence:

I have a little shadow that goes in and out with me and what can be the use of him is more than I can see.

1. This sentence may be hard to read because one comma has been left out. Where would you put a comma to break up the sentence into two main parts?
   a. After *shadow*
   b. After *me*
   c. After *him*
   d. After *more*
2. What kind of sentence is this?
   a. Simple
   b. Complex
   c. Compound
   d. Compound-complex
3. What is *I have a little shadow*?
   a. The subject of the sentence
   b. The first independent clause
   c. The first subordinate clause
   d. The subject of *him*

4. What is *and?*
   a. A coordinating conjunction
   b. A subordinating conjunction
   c. A relative pronoun
   d. A preposition modifying *what*
5. What is *and what can be the use of him?*
   a. The second independent clause
   b. A subordinate clause modifying *shadow*
   c. A subordinate clause, subject of *is*
   d. A subordinate clause, subject of *see*
6. What is *is?*
   a. Verb of second independent clause
   b. Verb of second subordinate clause
   c. Verb modifying *more*
   d. A verb that does not have a subject
7. What is *more?*
   a. A coordinating conjunction
   b. A subordinating conjunction
   c. An adverb modifying *than I can see*
   d. A linking-verb complement
8. What is the subject of the first independent clause?
   a. *I*
   b. *shadow*
   c. *I have a little shadow*
   d. *that goes in and out with me*
9. What is the subject of the second independent clause?
   a. *shadow*
   b. *that goes in and out with me*
   c. *what can be the use of him*
   d. *more than I can see*
10. How many subordinate clauses are there in this sentence?
   a. One
   b. Two
   c. Three
   d. Four
11. What is the subject of the first subordinate clause?
   a. *shadow*
   b. *that*
   c. *what*
   d. *more*

12. What is the verb of the first independent clause?
    a. *have*
    b. *goes*
    c. *can be*
    d. *can see*
13. What is *shadow?*
    a. Subject of the whole sentence
    b. Object of *have*
    c. A linking-verb complement
    d. Object of the preposition *little*
14. What does *with me* modify?
    a. *shadow*
    b. *have*
    c. *goes*
    d. *in and out*
15. What is *what?*
    a. A relative pronoun
    b. An interrogative pronoun
    c. An indefinite pronoun
    d. A personal pronoun
16. *Can be* is a different form of the same verb as
    a. *have*
    b. *goes*
    c. *is*
    d. *can see*
17. The subordinate clauses in this sentence have *three* of the following functions Which one do they *not* have?
    a. Noun
    b. Verb
    c. Adjective
    d. Adverb

—From P. B. Diederich (1974), Measuring Growth in English, *Urbana, IL: National Council of Teachers of English, 82–84.*

As soon as the students finish taking the exam, we review each item and discuss the answers right then in class. Since I don't have an answer key, we have to reach consensus about which choices are correct. Often we can't figure out the correct answer to a question, so we just skip that item and go on to the next one.

And then we talk about the test. Among the issues we discuss are questions such as

- "Is this what you want to prepare your students for? How much of this is worth knowing?"
- "Let's say that you actually get your students to the point where they can answer all these items correctly. Would you say that now your students are good writers?"

The students get the point that the knowledge of grammatical terms and sentence structure needed for successful completion of this test is overkill. Of course, students need *some* basic information about sentence structure and related items. By making the invisible visible—making students *aware* of certain basic features of grammar and usage—we can help them improve their ability to revise and edit their writing. But an overemphasis on grammar instruction can be detrimental: we tend to teach more than the students need to know, and it takes time away from other, more important aspects of writing instruction. If you want a comprehensive discussion of the issue about just how much and what kind of grammar instruction is necessary and desirable, you might read the volumes by Noguchi (1991) and Weaver (1996) that I have listed at the end of this chapter. They are both excellent sources of pertinent information and valuable insights.

At this point, I show the students the second part of the "exam" that is also included in Diederich's book (84):

Here is the sentence again:

I have a little shadow that goes in and out with me and what can be the use of him is more than I can see.

DIRECTIONS: Rewrite this sentence in as many of the following ways as you can. Use the same words that are in this sentence but change the form and order of these words as required. Try not to change or omit any of the ideas expressed by this sentence. Each rewritten version should be a single complete sentence.

18. Start with *I had a little shadow.*
19. Start with *I cannot see the use.*
20. Start with *The children had.*
21. Start with *Do you have.*
22. Start with *What can be the use.*
23. Start with *Going in and out with me.*
24. Start with *More than I can see.*

We do this part orally as I ask volunteers to compose and read aloud each new sentence above according to the directions. A student volunteer for number 18 will say, for example, "I *had* a little shadow that *went* in and out with me, and what *could* be the use of him *was* more than I could see." Students have little difficulty composing these sentences according to the directions given, and so we talk about that, too:

"How did you do that? How did you know what to change in the sentence so that you created a perfectly appropriate and acceptable revision?"

The insight illustrated by the above activity is that students generally already possess the knowledge of the grammatical structures and rules necessary to compose such sentences and engage in oral and written discourse. However, students still need practice with sentence strategies that take advantage of this prior knowledge, that allow students to build on what they already know and can do with language. This, then, became one of the goals of my grammar course—to introduce students to these kinds of alternative strategies, including sentence-combining and sentence-modeling activities.

Class Structure

I designed my grammar course with three goals in mind:

- Students should leave the class at the end of the semester knowing more about basic principles of grammar and usage than they knew when they entered.
- Students should be made aware of—and have opportunities to practice with—alternatives to traditional grammar instruction such as sentence-combining and sentence-modeling strategies.
- Students should be encouraged to play with language through creative writing activities, word games, and other forms of word play. In this way, students are provided opportunities to discover various features of the language and explore its possibilities for creative expression. In addition, students will gain some appropriate and engaging activities to use in their own classrooms.

Basic Knowledge

To achieve the first goal—increasing students' knowledge of basic grammatical terms, concepts, and structures—I arrange for students to give presentations throughout the semester that deal with various hard-core grammatical terms: simple, compound, and complex sentences; participles; gerbils; the marsupial clause; etc. Students get together with one or two other classmates and select which terms they'll learn and explain to the class. In this way, each student—or group of students—takes responsibility for teaching a part of the material to his or her classmates and, in turn, he or she will learn from others.

But there's the matter of making the presentations engaging and fun as well as worthwhile. Students must incorporate and display at least *two* of the following eleven elements:

The presentations must be

- musical;
- literary;
- colorful;
- visual; or
- edible.

They must involve

- movement;
- cartoons;
- a game;
- a newspaper;
- scissors, glue, and tape; or
- fantasy or make-believe.

In this way, students learn to design creative and engaging presentations dealing with grammar instruction. They have some additional guidelines to follow, standards that describe the characteristics of an outstanding presentation:

- You made learning happen. And you created a way to check and make sure that you did.
- Every member of the class is actively involved. They are doing more than simply listening to you.
- The activities are challenging, fun, and worthwhile.
- Handouts, information, and directions are clear and easy to understand.
- The presentation is well organized and has been well prepared.
- You have obviously done your homework and learned the material well yourself so that you could explain it to others.

Here are a couple of examples of presentations that students have created, incorporating some of those "strange and unnatural" elements listed above:

1. To begin her explanation of the structure of a *complex sentence,* a student brought in paper cups, filled them with milk, and handed a cup to each of her classmates.

"This milk is like an independent clause," she stated. "It can stand on its own. It is consumable all by itself."

Then she produced packages of powdered instant breakfast mix.

"By itself, it's just a powder and can't be consumed. It is *dependent* on the milk to become edible."

She then proceeded to pour the contents of a package into her cup of milk and stir the mixture together.

"Now we have assembled the structure of a complex sentence, created with both the dependent and independent elements."

2. Two students wanted to do a presentation about homonyms. They began with some standard explanations and clarification of the more common homonyms and then provided written exercises that allowed students to test their understanding of the material. For the final part of their presentation, however, they handed out oversized "Bingo" cards—except that, instead of numbers, each of the squares had homonyms printed on them. The presenters also handed out markers that their classmates could place on these squares at the appropriate moment during this game.

   The presenters then read aloud a series of sentences containing homonyms. If someone in the audience had that particular homonym—spelled appropriately—on his or her card, he or she placed a marker on that square.

   At the end of the game, it was easy to tell if we had chosen the correct spellings of all the homonyms used in the sentences. All we had to do was look at the pattern of the markers on the card: if our responses were correct, the pattern spelled out the letters of a homonym.

   The markers that we were given for this activity, by the way, were miniature peanut butter cups. So, we got to "eat our words" at the end of the game.

I've described the characteristics and structure of these presentations because I wanted to illustrate some ways to make grammar instruction engaging, effective, and fun for students. You might try adapting and using some of these strategies for other course content and student projects and see what happens. Create your own list of required elements—musical, literary, visual, etc.—for students' presentations. These elements could be incorporated into speeches that students would give in front of class to introduce themselves or a classmate; or into research projects, the results of which students would present to the whole class; or perhaps into alternative book reports or oral readings of texts.

Alternative Strategies

My second goal in the course is to introduce some worthwhile alternatives to traditional grammar instruction that my students can use in their own classrooms. These alternative strategies, including sentence-combining, sentence-modeling, and sentence-scrambling exercises, help students focus on stylistic matters in their writing. At each class session, the students practice one or more of these strategies, and we discuss the characteristics and benefits of each exercise we complete. At the end of this chapter, I have listed the titles of some valuable resources that deal with these strategies in some depth and present a wealth of examples and exercises for student practice.

Writing Activities

The students also complete some writing activities, all designed to encourage them to play with language—the third goal in the course—and to see grammar instruction as being something other than dreary, dark, and dull.

One assignment directs students to write a poem about a grammatical term or element. Following are a couple of students' responses:

The Comma
The comma,
   a tiny yield sign,
      whispering, "Slow down."
   a rest stop
      along the sentence of life.
   a pause for peace,
      for silence, for thought.
   a tiny buttressed dam
      between the surging flow of ideas.
   a pregnant belly
      birthing the next brilliant utterance.
   a cupped hand
      to hold on to the last precious one.
So often needed,
   too often abused
The comma,
   a scythe cutting through the literary jungle.
            —*Atuanya Cheatham*

"I Am" Poem
I am an adjective, I am colorful
I wonder what a sentence would be without me

I hear teachers calling for my use
I see my listings in a Thesaurus
I want to be included everywhere
I am an adjective, I am colorful

I pretend all writers will use me profusely
I feel I can be of so much assistance
I touch the nouns, pronouns and other adjectives I modify
I worry that without me, others will not know to what quality,
    quantity or extent
I cry when students ignore me
I am an adjective, I am colorful

I understand that not everyone knows my value
I say, try me more, I'll work for you
I dream of earning a Pulitzer Prize
I try to present myself properly
I hope to add to and modify well
I am an adjective, I am colorful

—*Linda Cashman*

A second writing activity involves students in writing a love letter or a letter of complaint to a particular verb tense. Two student examples:

My Dearest Past Tense,

I am afraid I must say goodbye. I need a present or even a future, but you are the past. Oh, my love, this is very difficult to write. What we had or should have will never be because there is no future. I cannot live this way. What was is over. What will be, will be. You need help, help that I cannot give. I have longing for a future. Please forgive me for writing. I cannot find you because you're past.

Sincerely,

Present with a Future

—*Joan Solomon*

Dearest Future Tense:

I look to you with inspiration as the tense that guarantees to be there for me tomorrow. You will always be moving forward and getting ahead—pursuing the unlimited future.

When I'm with you, my heart overflows with excitement about tomorrow. I am always challenged to improve and develop into the person I want to be in the future.

With you, there is no looking back. Your wide vision and magical mystery keep me desperately yearning for the future—a future filled with unexpected surprises and enchantments. Yes, you will be my prize.

Never again will I have to wonder what happened in the past, what could have happened yesterday, or what may be happening as we speak. Your strength and enthusiasm for what will be keeps me forever in your love.

May we face tomorrow together and forever. The past is gone forever. The present is fleeting. But the future can be planned for in advance,
waited for in expectation,
hoped for with childish excitement,
lived for with unabashed vigor.

—*Judy Castillo*

A third writing prompt directs students: "Assume the role of either a prosecutor or a defense attorney. Write your opening statement to the jury, summarizing the case against the prisoner. The prisoner is a dependent clause." A student example:

To the Honorable Judge Verbal of the Division of Language Courts of the United States of Grammarica, and to all the dependent clauses of the jury: I, State Prosecuting Attorney John Participle, am standing here this morning to tell you that the defendant in this case against the State, Dependent Clause, "Because you were here," has violated a cardinal rule of the Code of Grammatical Ethics, Section DC of Code SS, which states that dependent clauses cannot stand alone in a sentence. During the course of this trial, I will show you how "Because you were here" posed as a sentence, positioning himself on the pages of compositions and essays found in elementary schools and university campuses alike. You will hear from key witnesses, namely English teachers and newspaper editors, of how this dependent clause was seen blatantly standing alone in compositions and newspaper articles, causing confusion and lack of clarity and eventually wiping away the dignity and credibility of otherwise decent pieces of writing. Jury members, it will be your duty to listen to these witnesses and examine the writing samples presented, however difficult it may be. I am confident that you will come to the only plausible verdict, "guilty as charged." Help me ensure the erasure or deletion of this maverick dependent clause so that he will never again mar the pages of aspiring writers throughout Grammarica. Thank you.

—*Melanie Batista*

Other writing activities that invite students to play with language include:

- Design a magazine ad selling a verb.
- Write an obituary notice for a grammatical term, including a summary of its accomplishments in life.
- Yesterday's newspaper headline was about a grammatical term. What did it say?

- Explain how the transmodal pluperfect auxiliary verb tense works and give examples. (No, I don't know how it works, either. The students have to invent this one.)

Word Play

Besides completing the writing activities, students play with language in other ways to explore its possibilities for creative expression. They play with similes, metaphors, puns, riddles, cliches, euphemisms, and ambiguities in language. The "Dear John" letter that opened this chapter is one example of such word play. These creative and engaging activities make the invisible features of language visible to students, expanding students' range of options that they can employ in their own language use and communication efforts.

Richard Lederer's books serve as valuable resources for this kind of word play. He offers language games, puzzles, and other interesting and worthwhile strategies, and I have listed some of his books at the end of the chapter. Following is one example of the kinds of word play that Lederer offers students in his texts.

Metaphors in Our Language   In his clever and insightful *book The Play of Words: Fun & Games for Language Lovers* (1990), Lederer invites students to brainstorm common phrases in our language that involve a metaphorical reference to *anatomical parts*:

- *eye* of a needle;
- your *neck* of the woods;
- a *head* of lettuce;
- the *heart* of the matter, etc.

Hold a brainstorming session with students and generate as many of these phrases as you can think of. Keep a list posted on the classroom wall and invite students to add items to the list as they think of them. Start each day of class with these kinds of brainstorming sessions. Have students create a list of common phrases that involve a metaphorical use of *colors*:

- singing the *blues*;
- caught *red*-handed;
- silence is *golden*;
- every cloud has a *silver* lining, etc.

. . . and the *weather*:

- shoot the *breeze*;
- eggs *sunny*-side up;

- *gales* of laughter;
- steal someone's *thunder*, etc.

. . . and metaphorical references to animals; clothes; music; etc. Through these activities, students make sense of the structure and possibilities of language in ways that make sense to them.

So What?

As the end of the semester approaches, I want to find out if learning has happened for my students in this class. More importantly, I want the students themselves to become aware of what learning—if any—has occurred. Sure, we had fun with the student presentations and the writing activities and the word play, and the students experienced sentence-combining and other worthwhile strategies. But what did they learn? Did any of these activities make a difference to them? To find out, I ask the students to write a reflective paper in which they respond to these two questions[2]:

- So what?
- Now what?

Here are excerpts from students' papers:

I find it liberating to know that the research gives me permission to place less emphasis on teaching formal grammar. Freeing up this time by using mini–grammar lessons will allow more time to practice writing.

For me, this class has given a set of new ideas to take the place of some very "dead horses." This class has been a model of a way to use activities, like sentence-combining, to show students ways to improve and enhance writing. The fact that playing with words can be fun should stimulate a more positive attitude toward students' writing. The more that writing is practiced, the more readily students will approximate correctness, interest and variety in their writing.

—Linda Cashman

I believe that these activities have opened my mind to other possible assignments in the classroom. As a student, I always felt that learning grammar had to entail either circling or underlining bits of grammatical mush or using the "wonderful" device of the diagram for every sentence under the rainbow. Really, I think that these interactive assignments would really facilitate the students towards their/my learning goals. In other words, assignments don't have to be boring in order to have learning happen. Also, the exercises presented in class really would foster a community of learners. In today's society, this goal is optimal.

—Elizabeth Tuten

Another time, I used a different set of questions to engage the students in reflection on their learning during the semester:

- What did you learn?
- How do you know?

Some excerpts from students' papers:

Perhaps the most valuable thing I learned in this class is that learning depends heavily on the way in which the material is presented. This class allowed me to experience a wide variety of teaching styles, and although some were better than others, all were open for debate. It was during these debates that I really think that learning happened for me.

—*Robert Counts*

Although I did not learn anything "new" about grammar rules this semester, I learned a lot about learning and teaching grammar. At times I was frustrated because I was not attending a class that was wrapped up neatly in a little box, waiting for me to untie the bow on top. You see, that's how most of my classes are presented. I may not always know what the teacher is going to teach me, but I know how to spit the material back at the professor in the manner expected. This grammar class was different. It was different because the parameters for most assignments were undefined. You asked me to be creative, and I am not used to that. You asked me what I thought of your assignments, and I am definitely not used to that. Finally, you listened to my opinions, and again, I am not used to that. I realized that learning can be fun, and the more fun I had with the assignments, the less they seemed like assignments. . . .

This semester I learned a lot about learning as well [as] teaching. I think I finally figured out what you mean when you say "make learning happen." It certainly happened for me!

—*Kelly Jacobson*

Through this reflective assessment, students focus on the ways in which this course has influenced their thoughts about grammar instruction. They also reflect on how this influence will affect their teaching when they have their own classrooms and are faced with the issues identified earlier: How much grammar should be taught? When should it be taught? And how can it be taught in ways that are effective and engaging?

Notes

1. The "Dear John" letter was created by Gloria Rosenthal and published in *Games Magazine* (January 1984): 59. Reprinted with permission of Gloria Rosenthal and *Games Magazine*; all rights reserved.

Punctuated one way, the "Dear John" letter becomes a love note:

Dear John,

I want a man who knows what love is all about. You are generous, kind, thoughtful. People who are not like you admit to being useless and inferior, John. You have ruined me for other men. I yearn for you. I have no feelings whatsoever when we're apart. I can be forever happy. Will you let me be yours?

—*Gloria*

But, punctuated another way, the "Dear John" letter changes to a "get-lost" message:

Dear John,

I want a man who knows what love is. All about you are generous, kind, thoughtful people who are not like you. Admit to being useless and inferior, John. You have ruined me. For other men, I yearn. For you, I have no feelings whatsoever. When we're apart, I can be forever happy. Will you let me be? Yours,

—*Gloria*

2. The idea of using the two questions "So what?" and "Now what?" for reflection arose from conversations the author had with Dr. Stephen Marcus (University of California, Santa Barbara) and from Stephen Marcus' article "What? So What? Now What?" in *Computers, Reading, and Language Arts* (Winter 1984/1985): 7–8.

Recommended Readings and Resources

Daiker, D., A. Kerek, M. Morenberg, and J. Sommers. 1994. *The Writer's Options: Combining to Composing.* 5th ed. New York: HarperCollins College.

Diederich, P. B. 1974. *Measuring Growth in English.* Urbana, IL: National Council of Teachers of English.

Killgallon, D. 1997. *Sentence Composing for Middle School: A Worktext on Sentence Variety and Maturity.* Portsmouth, NH: Boynton/Cook.

———. 1998. *Sentence Composing for High School: A Worktext on Sentence Variety and Maturity.* Portsmouth, NH: Boynton/Cook.

Lederer, R. 1990. *The Play of Words: Fun & Games for Language Lovers.* New York: Simon & Schuster.

———. 1994. *Adventures of a Verbivore.* New York: Simon & Schuster.

Marcus, S. "What? So What? Now What?" *Computers, Reading, and Language Arts* (Winter 1984/1985): 7–8.

Noden, H. 1999. *Image Grammar: Using Grammatical Structures to Teach Writing.* Portsmouth, NH: Boynton/Cook.

Noguchi, R. R. 1991. *Grammar and the Teaching of Writing: Limits and Possibilities.* Urbana, IL: National Council of Teachers of English.

Weaver, C. 1996. *Teaching Grammar in Context.* Portsmouth, NH: Boynton/Cook.

———, ed. 1998. *Lessons to Share on Teaching Grammar in Context.* Portsmouth, NH: Boynton/Cook.

6

Lesson Planning: Putting It All Together

Certainly an important part of making learning happen for students is designing instructional activities that are challenging, engaging, worthwhile, and fun. But what is still needed is an overview—a structure, a framework—that will enable you to put it all together. Decisions need to be made about where you're going with these activities, what you're trying to accomplish, and perhaps most importantly, how you will know when you have achieved your objective. This is what lesson planning is all about. The purpose of this chapter, then, is to suggest a course of action you might follow in your lesson-planning efforts.

The World's Simplest Lesson Plan

There are lots of different forms for lesson plans, but they all deal with four basic issues. Whether you're trying to decide what to do in class next Monday or mapping out a monthlong thematic unit of study, if you address these four basic questions as part of your lesson-planning efforts, you will have created the blueprint you need for your classroom instruction:

Question 1: *Where do you want to go?*
What is it exactly that you want to accomplish?

Question 2: *Why do you want to go there?*
Why is this an especially important and relevant and worthwhile instructional goal to pursue?

Question 3: *How will you get there?*
What instructional strategies and activities will you use? What will the students be doing in class? In what sequence?

How will they complete these activities? In small groups? Individually? What prior skills will they need to have mastered in order to complete the activities successfully?

Question 4:   *How will you know when you have arrived?*

How will you determine that the instruction "worked" and that you accomplished what you set out to do? How will the students demonstrate that they are now "new and improved" as a result of having completed this activity or project or sequence of strategies?

Where Do You Want to Go?

Imagine for a moment that you are planning to take a well-deserved vacation. You have a week's free time coming up, and you want to travel somewhere. Great! But, what's the first decision you have to make?

"Where do I want to go?"

All your vacation planning depends on your answer to this question. Your decision about where you want to go will determine whether you will order plane tickets or gas up the car or get your bicycle tuned up. It will determine what clothes you will pack and what else you will take with you. It will give you a good idea about how much money you will need and what reservations you will need to make.

Lesson planning proceeds in much the same way, beginning with your response to the question "What is it I want to accomplish?" Your answer will determine much of what happens subsequently in the classroom. *To ignore this question is to risk mistaking motion for progress.* Certainly you can just go ahead and create lots of classroom activities that will keep the students busy during the day or the week. But, once the students have finished their worksheets or reading or whatever else you have assigned them, what then? What has been accomplished? Where do the students go from here?

Robert F. Mager, in his book *Preparing Instructional Objectives* (1962), states the problem this way: ". . . if you're not sure where you're going, you're liable to end up someplace else—and not even know it" (vii). I would add a corollary to his statement: "If you're not sure where you're going, how will you know when you have arrived?"

This is where the various published lists of standards can be helpful. Most states have established standards for classroom instruction, and the National Council of Teachers of English has also published its own comprehensive list of standards. These standards serve as blueprints of desired destinations for your instructional journeys. They identify worthwhile and expected goals, often phrasing the objectives in terms of "what the students should know and be able to do."

97

The Florida Department of Education, as one example, has published its Sunshine State Standards. The standards are presented in a hierarchical structure:

Subject area: domain, content area, such as language arts, mathematics, science, music

    Strand: label (word or short phrase) for a category of knowledge, such as reading, writing, culture, nature of matter

        Standard: general statement of expected learner achievement

            Benchmark: learner expectations (what a student should know and be able to do) at the end of the developmental levels of grades Pre-K–2, 3–5, 6–8, 9–12.

                Sample Performance Descriptions: examples of things a student could do to demonstrate achievement of the benchmark.

Here is a representative example of the kind of content one will find at each of these levels of specificity in the Sunshine State Standards. This example appears among the standards listed for grades 9–12 in *Florida Curriculum Framework: Language Arts* (1996, 50):

Subject Area:	Language Arts
Strand:	Reading
Standard:	The student constructs meaning from a wide range of texts.
Benchmark:	Determines the author's purpose and point of view and their effects on the text.
Sample Performance Descriptions:	Presents an analysis of stereotyping, bias, propaganda, and contrasting points of view in material read. Reads an essay to determine the author's point of view and makes a personal determination of the validity of the author's argument.

Whether you set your own standards and goals or use your district's or state's standards as a resource, you need to address this issue directly, clearly, and immediately in your lesson planning. Decide where you want to go in your instruction—"What is it that I want to accomplish?"—and the rest of your planning will begin to fall into place.

Why Do You Want to Go There?

A related question that will affect your decision about where you want to go is "Why do I want to go there?" Why is this an especially relevant and important activity or skill for your students to engage in or master? Your students are asking you this same question whenever they ask: "Why do we have to do this?" You owe them an answer, one that makes sense . . . both to them and to you.

Sometimes this decision is made *for* us. For instance, the district mandates that a certain goal, activity, or course of study will be included and taught; or your departmental colleagues have all agreed that certain topics and skills must be "covered." In such cases, you might try to find ways to integrate these items into your own curriculum and structure, which will enable you and your students to work on them with enthusiasm and commitment.

How Will You Get There?

Once you have decided where you want to go with your instruction, you can then turn to the matter of mapping a route of instructional strategies that will get you there. You want this route—this sequence and structure of activities—to be engaging, to allow students to be active participants in their own learning. This is where the principles of an interactive classroom can be helpful. Design and structure activities in such a way that

- Students are performing with language.
- Cooperative learning is encouraged.
- Students are engaging in authentic communication. This means they are speaking and writing to real audiences for real purposes.
- The focus of the activities is on constructing, comprehending, negotiating, and communicating meanings.

A similar list of desired characteristics of classroom instruction appears in a new volume published by Harvey Daniels and Marilyn Bizar, *Methods That Matter: Six Structures for Best Practice Classrooms* (1998). They point out that Best Practice classrooms exhibit and incorporate certain features recommended by "the many standards projects . . . emerging from professional associations, research centers, and curriculum groups around the country" (2). These features—what Daniels and Bizar identify as the six basic structures—include

- integrative units;
- small-group activities;
- representing-to-learn;

- classroom workshop;
- authentic experiences; and
- reflective assessment.

Classrooms that exhibit these structures, according to Daniels and Bizar, are

- student-centered;
- experiential;
- reflective;
- authentic;
- holistic;
- social;
- collaborative;
- democratic;
- cognitive;
- developmental;
- constructivist; and
- challenging.

Some of the six structures above echo the principles of an interactive classroom. The important point is that in your lesson-planning efforts, you should try to incorporate these principles and structures. Having decided where you want to go in your instruction, you can use these ways of structuring classroom interaction to help you and your students get there.

How Will You Know When You Have Arrived?

In addition to deciding where you want to go and mapping an appropriate route to get there, you need to address the issue of how you will determine when you (and your students) have "arrived." How will you know that the students are now new and improved as a result of their having completed the assigned task—the writing, the reading, the group work, the term project, even the whole semester's course? Will you give an exam? Assign a culminating project or essay? Require a performance of some sort? Whatever else you do, be sure to include one or more reflective assessment activities. They're designed to let you—and equally important, your *students*—know that *progress* has been made, that significant learning has indeed happened. And, if it *hasn't* happened, the reflective work will let you know that, too.

Two Lesson-Planning Efforts

When It All Fits Together

Many of the activities in this volume and also in my 1994 book, *Activities for an Interactive Classroom*, were designed, assembled, and sequenced as part of various lesson-planning efforts. To illustrate how these activities are responsive to the questions posed in "The World's Simplest Lesson Plan," let me use as an example the instructional unit and series of activities dealing with giving directions clearly (see pages 39–52).

"Where Do I Want to Go?" All of the activities in this unit are designed to develop students' ability to give directions clearly in either the oral or written modes. This is "where I want to go"—what I want to accomplish— with this unit.

"Why Do I Want to Go There?" The rationale for this unit—"why I want to go there"—may be found in a couple of places. Various standards established by both state and national organizations, for instance, identify goals pertinent to this unit. Among the NCTE and the International Reading Association's standards for the English language arts are these two goals:

- Students adjust their use of spoken, written, and visual language (e.g., conventions, style, vocabulary) to communicate effectively with a variety of audiences and for different purposes.
- Students employ a wide range of strategies as they write and use different writing process elements appropriately to communicate with different audiences for a variety of purposes. (*Standards for the English Language Arts*, 1996, 25)

Among Florida's Sunshine State Standards, moreover, is an extensive list of benchmarks—learner performance expectations—dealing with the following goal: "The student writes to communicate ideas and information effectively" (Florida State Department of Education 1996, 63–70).

These standards are worth pursuing, and an instructional unit aimed at developing students' ability to give directions clearly seems to be one way to meet these standards. Another answer to the "Why do I want to go there?" question may be found in the Speech Communication Association's identification of the basic functional communication competencies. In the SCA-sponsored volume *Development of Functional Communication Competencies: Grades 7–12*, the editor, Barbara Wood, notes, "A number of theorists have sorted communication acts into broad categories of acts—sets of communication acts which are basically similar to each other in overall communicative purpose. The term 'communication functions' is used to refer to these categories of communication purposes (acts). There are basically five communication functions . . ." (1977, 3–4). Wood then identifies these five communication functions as *controlling, feeling, informing, ritualizing,* and *imagining.* About the informing function, Wood says, "These are communication acts in which the participants' function is to offer or seek information; for example, stating information, questioning, answering, justifying, naming, pointing out an object, demonstrating, explaining, and acknowledging" (4).

The "Giving Directions Clearly" instructional unit, then, serves as an integral means of improving students' competence in this basic *informative* function of communication.

"How Will I Get There?"   Each of the activities in the instructional sequence as described on pages 34–57 is aimed squarely at the skill of giving directions clearly. Some of them engage students in oral communication and others involve the writing mode. But it is important to note that I am not trying to "cover" this skill or objective. I am not simply trying to "get through" this unit of instruction so that I can then move on to something else. We hear this particular verb *cover* used a lot in schools, as in "I've got to cover adverbial clauses this week" or "Have you covered poetry yet this semester?" The assumption seems to be that once you've covered this subject or that skill, it has been done—it has been taken care of . . . forever!

My own approach, however, is quite different: I try to UN-*cover* the material or skill at hand. I will design and assemble and conduct several activities, each of which is focused on the same skill or material but develops the subject a little bit more and makes the information a little bit clearer. In this way, I "UN-cover" the subject for the students. With each activity or experience in the unit, the student learns a little more and becomes more insightful and more competent in his or her communication efforts. Instead of covering a subject, I engage students in exploring and experiencing that subject in a variety of ways.

This, then, is the purpose of the several activities dealing with giving directions clearly. Some of the activities—such as the "Airport" exercise and the "One-Way Versus Two-Way Communication" activity—simply allow students to assess their own, current level of direction-giving abilities. They also serve to make students consciously aware of the nature and complexity of this skill. Other activities follow that engage students in practicing and rehearsing their direction-giving abilities. All the activities, however, incorporate the principles of an *interactive* approach: students are performing with language; using their own talk as a means of learning; and communicating to a real audience for a real purpose.

"How Will I Know When I Have Arrived?"   Finally, there are the "proof-of-purchase" activities at the end, the exercises that require students to demonstrate their new and improved communication competence. For the "Giving Directions Clearly" unit, I utilize final, performance activities that engage students in a demonstration of their competence in both the oral and written modes. Students' successful completion of these final activities—the Demonstration Talk (see pages 40–47) and the "Giving Directions Clearly" writing activity task (see pages 40–44)—demonstrates that significant learning has happened.

When You Really Have to Work at It

Planning the instructional sequence on giving directions clearly was fairly straight-forward: The objective is clear; the rationale is solid and evident; and the activities are appropriate, engaging, and worthwhile. It's a pretty neat and tidy package of planning there.

But, lesson planning doesn't always proceed that smoothly. Sometimes you are told specifically what to teach and must struggle to find a valid reason to teach it; other times you try to deal directly and deeply with a subject or skill but find in the end that you have simply covered it. You focused the students' attention and efforts on memorizing definitions or identifying key items, but in the end, you realize that no time was spent on any authentic meaning-making activities. So, you are left wondering if any significant learning happened at all.

At still other times, you might have heard about an idea that seems like a great strategy and you want to try it out in the classroom, but you're not exactly sure what it's designed to accomplish. Should you run it anyway and risk mistaking motion for progress?

I want to describe for you now one of those messy lesson-planning efforts, one of those times when I couldn't easily provide ready answers to the four basic lesson-planning questions. By re-creating my thinking that occurred during this particular lesson-planning effort, I can show you a more realistic picture of how lesson-planning often proceeds.

Each week, my methods class meets on-site at a local high school, and for part of the class session, I conduct demonstration lessons and activities involving both my methods students and the high school students in one of the school's English classes. At the beginning of the semester, the school's English teachers had signed up their classes for these collaborative sessions, so I knew in advance which class I'd be working with each week. Several days in advance of each week's session, I would call the teacher whose class was scheduled next and obtain some pertinent information: "What are you working on now with your students?", "Is there a particular kind of lesson or activity you'd like to see?", etc.

During one of these phone calls, the teacher mentioned that she would like to see me do something with two poems that she had to "cover" in the textbook the next week. (Uh-oh! There's that word again.) Evidently, her class was dealing with American literature that semester, and these poems were the next items to be covered in her curriculum.

"Okay, I'll come out to the school and get a copy of your textbook and see what I can do," I said. "How's that?"

So I visited her class, picked up a copy of the textbook, and learned which poems she wanted me to cover in my demonstration lesson. They were Stephen

Crane's "War Is Kind" and Walt Whitman's "Beat! Beat! Drums!" I opened the book, found the poems, and stared. Sure, I had seen them before, but they just lay there on the page that day, staring back at me blankly. This, I could tell, would be a challenge. That evening, the lesson planning began in earnest:

Okay, so we've got these two "war" poems here. Could do the "Three Questions" activity—"Write down three questions you have about these poems. Now assemble into small groups and get answers to your questions."

But I had used that strategy in a previous demonstration lesson some weeks before. The methods students knew about that one, and they needed to see some new and different instructional techniques in action. I knew that whatever I did, the students needed to engage in constructing and negotiating meanings; they needed to communicate to a real audience for real purposes; and they should talk more than I would. Whatever else I accomplished, I wanted the experience to be both meaningful and memorable.

Maybe I could focus on the tone of voice in these poems. And the theme of war. That has possibilities.

Then I remembered some other, similar poems about war that I had worked with in the past, for instance, "There Will Come Soft Rains" by Sara Teasdale. I had read aloud the short story of the same title by Ray Bradbury and then had had the students look closely at the poem. The big questions at the end of the discussion were "Why did Bradbury borrow the title of the poem for his short story? How are these two literary works similar?"

I had also worked with Carl Sandburg's poem "Grass," instructing students to compare it with Teasdale's poem above because the two share a similar perspective. And finally, there was Wilfred Owen's war poem, "Dulce et Decorum Est." Nothing subtle about that one!

Okay, so now I've got a total of five poems on the subject of war. What'll I do with them? Maybe I could get the students to assemble in small groups and give each group a different poem. No, wait! There'll be more than five groups, certainly. Well, it's okay if two groups have the same poem. Shouldn't pose a problem.

Let's have the students in their groups read the poems aloud to the class. I'll tell them to read it in such a way as to bring out whatever meaning they find in it. So they'll need to look closely at the text to decide who should read which line and how it should be read.

But how will they determine that meaning that they're supposed to convey in their reading? And the appropriate tone of voice? Need something more here, something that has to come before the reading—some kind of preparation work.

So I built in some preliminary steps—two tasks that the groups of students should complete before they began preparing their oral reading of their poem:

1. The students should prepare a concise summary of the poem itself—a brief statement of "Here's what the poem is about" or "Here's what happens in the poem." This statement would be given orally to the class as an introduction to the oral presentation.

2. The students need to gain insight into the theme of the poem. But it's one thing to instruct students to "find the theme," and a whole different matter to actually *teach* this skill. So, I decided to direct students to complete the following steps as a way to accomplish this task:

   a. Divide a sheet of paper in half lengthwise so that there are two columns. Label the top of the left column, "What is the poem about?" and the top of the right column, "What is the author saying about it?"

   b. List as many items as you think appropriate in the left column . . . but for *each* item you list, you must fill in the corresponding space in the right-hand column.

   c. When you have finished filling in the two columns, write a sentence in which you combine the ideas in both halves of the columns. These are the *themes* of the poem. Your sentence will identify the things that the author is dealing with and describe what he or she is saying about those things.

At this point, I stood back and examined my sequence of activities in light of the questions posed by "The World's Simplest Lesson Plan":

Okay, so what have I got now? The students, working in small groups, will prepare an oral reading of the poem. But they will introduce their reading with a summary or overview of the poem and a statement of the theme. So, what has been accomplished by these activities? We've got writing concisely; reading for the main idea; and identification of theme. And, through the groups' preparation of the poem for an oral reading, they'll be looking closely at the text, deciding how it should be read and by whom. That will involve constructing and negotiating meanings and certainly an examination of tone. Those are certainly all worthwhile skills and objectives. Yeah, this might work.

But there was still something missing, I realized. Where was the "proof-of-purchase" activity at the end, something to engage the students in reflecting on some aspect of the text or experience? Something was needed to help the students connect with these themes and poems, to see them as relevant to their own lives. Otherwise, it would just be "motion." The students would do the activities, of course—and yes, they were worthwhile—but then, there would remain the two questions "So what?" and "Now what?" Where do the students go from here?

And then I saw it!

The problem was that in the sequence as planned, students would be working with only one of the five poems. Oh, sure, they would hear an oral reading of the other four poems, and they would also learn a little bit about the poems' meanings and tone, but they would never *see* them and have an opportunity to work with them as well.

What if, after all the oral readings were completed, I handed out copies of all the poems to all the students? Then I could instruct the students to write a reflective paper on "Which of the poems comes closest to your own view of war?"

My lesson was planned.

A Final Word

There is an awful lot of *noise* and *nonsense* that clouds our work in the classroom. We feel as if we are being pulled in ten different directions. We try to meet the demands of the administrators and legislators to raise test scores, while at the same time we work feverishly to "cover the curriculum" and please the community that is overly concerned with the more visible aspects of writing instruction. Somewhere, buried deeply beneath all these demands and pressures, is our sincere desire to make meaningful and memorable learning happen for our students.

This is what I have tried to do in this volume: to put aside all the noise and nonsense for a moment and focus exclusively on what's worth knowing and doing in the classroom and how students learn. I have tried to show that you need to incorporate certain elements and principles into your instruction. You need to establish a positive classroom community, design and direct engaging activities, and provide an opportunity for your students to reflect on the learning that has occurred.

Moreover, instead of trying to cover the curriculum with its fifty-seven goals and objectives, you might keep yourself—and your students—focused on the one fundamental goal: improving students' performance with language. When you strip away all the noise and the nonsense, this is all that matters.

Well, actually, that's not entirely true. There *is* one other goal that matters, too, and it is hinted at in this poem:

To David, About His Education
The world is full of mostly invisible things,
And there is no way but putting the mind's eye,

Or its nose, in a book, to find them out,
Things like the square root of Everest
Or how many times Byron goes into Texas,
Or whether the law of the excluded middle
Applies west of the Rockies. For these
And the like reasons, you have to go to school
And study books and listen to what you are told,
And sometimes try to remember. Though I don't know
What you will do with the mean annual rainfall
On Plato's Republic, or the calorie content
Of the Diet of Worms, such things are said to be
Good for you, and you will have to learn them
In order to become one of the grown-ups
Who sees invisible things neither steadily nor whole,
But keeps gravely the grand confusion of the world
Under his hat, which is where it belongs,
And teaches small children to do this in their turn.

—*Howard Nemerov (1962, 54)*

It seems that our job as educators—our second goal—is to help our students come to see "invisible things" steadily and whole. And I wish you every success in your efforts to make this kind of learning happen.

Works Cited

Daniels, H. and M. Bizar. 1998. *Methods That Matter: Six Structures for Best Practice Classrooms.* York, ME: Stenhouse.

Florida State Department of Education. 1996. *Florida Curriculum Framework: Language Arts: Pre-K–12 Sunshine State Standards and Instructional Practices.* Tallahassee: Florida State Department of Education.

Mager, R. F. 1962. *Preparing Instructional Objectives.* Palo Alto, CA: Fearon.

Nemerov, H. 1962. *The Next Room of the Dream.* Chicago, IL: University of Chicago Press.

Standards for the English Language Arts. 1996. Urbana, IL: National Council of Teachers of English and the International Reading Association.

Wood, B. S., ed. 1977. *Development of Functional Communication Competencies: Grades 7–12.* Urbana, IL: ERIC Clearinghouse on Reading and Communication Skills and Speech Communication Association.

Index